P9-AZW-318

THE COMMUNIST MANIFESTO

Karl Marx and Friedrich Engels

With an Introduction by
Martin Malia
and a New Afterword by
Stephen Kotkin

SIGNET CLASSICS

SIGNET CLASSICS
Published by New American Library, a division of
Penguin Group (USA) Inc., 375 Hudson Street,
New York, New York 10014, USA
Penguin Group (Canada), 90 Eglinton Avenue East, Suite 700, Toronto,
Ontario M4P 2Y3, Canada (a division of Pearson Penguin Canada Inc.)
Penguin Books Ltd., 80 Strand, London WC2R 0RL, England
Penguin Ireland, 25 St. Stephen's Green, Dublin 2,
Ireland (a division of Penguin Books Ltd.)
Penguin Group (Australia), 250 Camberwell Road, Camberwell, Victoria 3124,
Australia (a division of Pearson Australia Group Pty. Ltd.)
Penguin Books India Pvt. Ltd., 11 Community Centre, Panchsheel Park,
New Delhi - 110 017, India
Penguin Group (NZ), 67 Apollo Drive, Rosedale, North Shore 0632,
New Zealand (a division of Pearson New Zealand Ltd.)
Penguin Books (South Africa) (Pty.) Ltd., 24 Sturdee Avenue,
Rosebank, Johannesburg 2196, South Africa

Penguin Books Ltd., Registered Offices:
80 Strand, London WC2R 0RL, England

Published by Signet Classics, an imprint of New American Library,
a division of Penguin Group (USA) Inc.

First Signet Classics Printing, October 1998
First Signet Classics Printing (Kotkin Afterword), May 2011
20 19 18 17 16 15 14 13 12

 REGISTERED TRADEMARK — MARCA REGISTRADA

Printed in the United States of America

Karl Marx (1818–1883) was born in Trier to a German Jewish family that had converted to Christianity. As a student he was influenced by Hegel's dialectical philosophy but later reacted against his mentor's idealism and turned instead to the then new socialist movement. *The Communist Manifesto* (utilizing drafts by his friend Friedrich Engels) was written in Brussels for a German emigré society, the Communist League. After taking part in the failed revolutions of 1848, Marx fled to London, where he and his family lived in poverty alleviated only by Engels' financial help. For some years, Marx was a London correspondent for a New York newspaper. He spent most of his time, however, researching in the British Museum to document his theories of class struggle and the "internal contradictions" undermining capitalism. His works include *The Poverty of Philosophy*, *The Eighteenth Brumaire of Louis Bonaparte*, *The German Ideology*, and *A Contribution to the Critique of Political Economy*.

Friedrich Engels (1820–1895) was born in Germany, the son of a textile manufacturer. After his military training in Berlin, he became an agent of his father's business in Manchester and immersed himself in Chartism and the problems of the new urban proletariat created by the industrial revolution. In 1844, the year he met Karl Marx, he wrote *The Condition of the Working Class in England*. The pair's ideas were incorporated into *The Communist Manifesto*. After Marx's death, Engels continued his work on *Das Kapital* and completed it in 1894, a year before his own death. He also wrote *The Peasant War in Germany*, *The Origin of the Family*, and *Socialism, Utopian and Scientific*.

Martin Malia did his undergraduate work at Yale and earned his PhD at Harvard. He has spent most of his teaching career at the University of California at Berkeley. His principal works include *Alexander Herzen and the Birth of Russian Socialism, 1812–1855*, *The Soviet Tragedy: A History of Socialism in Russia, 1917–1991*, and *Russia Under Western Eyes: From the Bronze Horseman to the Lenin Mausoleum*.

Stephen Kotkin teaches history and international affairs at Princeton. His books include *Armageddon Averted: The Soviet Collapse 1970–2000* and *Uncivil Society: 1989 and the Implosion of the Communist Establishment*. He formerly directed Princeton's Russian and Eurasian studies program (1996–2009) and served as the regular business book reviewer for the *New York Times* Sunday Business section (2006–2008). He founded and runs Princeton's Global History initiative.

CONTENTS

INTRODUCTION

When the *Manifesto of the Communist Party* was published on the eve of the February Revolution of 1848 in Paris, its principal author, Karl Marx, then barely thirty, was convinced that the triumph of his cause was imminent: the proletariat was about to "rise to the position of ruling class" in France, England, and Germany, and its victory worldwide was only a matter of time. One hundred and fifty years later, of course, these fantasies have proved to be just that. Yet it took almost that long for this to be demonstrated beyond a reasonable doubt; and meanwhile the Communist Specter he invoked in truth never ceased to haunt the world.

The sesquicentennial of the *Manifesto*, then, raises two questions: why did its prophesies appear so alluring to so many for so long; and why did they ultimately prove to be so hollow, even perverse? Since the specter has now been cast on the "ashheap of history" (where Trotsky consigned Bolshevism's adversaries in October 1917), the answer is best pursued by tracing its quite unexpected migrations from the advanced

West to the backward East, and from the revolutionary "springtime of 1848" to the twilight of utopia-in-power in 1989–91.

I: THE PATH TO THE *MANIFESTO*

It is the convention to explain Marxism's founding document as a response to the human costs of the Industrial Revolution; and this is indeed part of the story. But just as important is the conjunction of the new market society with the ideological heritage of the French Revolution: nascent industrialism, after all, was at its most advanced in England, whereas the epicenter of emerging socialism was France. It is less often emphasized, however, that the variant of socialism the *Manifesto* called "Communist" was produced by a pair of intellectuals, and that they hailed from then-preindustrial Germany.

Of course, Marx himself pointed out that his system was a synthesis of British political economy, French socialism, and German philosophy. Even so, until the discovery of his early manuscripts in the 1930s, it did not become clear that the German element of his amalgam was not only the first in time, but the most basic in substance.

Briefly put, classical German philosophy was an Idealism in which "the world conformed to mind" (in Kant's phrase), whereas the Anglo-French Enlightenment against which it was reacting was an empiricism in which mind conformed to the world. With Hegel, moreover, philosophy for the first time became historical in its essence, and truth was now a perpetual unfolding rather than a set system. In general terms, Marx sought to make this metaphysical historicism once again empirical by transforming it into a social science in the Anglo-French manner, or what he called "historical materialism."

As a "Left-Hegelian," Marx's starting point was Hegel's vision of history as the progression of "rationality" through dialectical negation and transcendence to "absolute" self-consciousness, a culmination which also signifies human freedom. Marx then assigned to this process the leveling goals and the commitment to "class struggle" of revolutionary French socialism. Finally, he made Hegel's conceptual logic materialistic by recasting it in a "critical" adaptation of the economic categories of Adam Smith and David Ricardo. Yet in the resulting system, the key component—the element which made it a system and gave it its allure—was the overarching "logic" of German philosophy.

Marx effected this synthesis during his first emigration, in Paris and Brussels, between 1843 and 1846. Simultaneously, he began his collaboration with Engels, who brought to the mix first-hand acquaintance with advanced English industrialism. And so, by 1846, in *The German Ideology* (their joint settling of accounts with Hegelianism, unpublished until 1932) all the essential elements of future Marxism had been fused.

At the same time, the pair were engaged in organizing émigré German workers in Paris, Brussels and London to prepare for an expected German revolution. In 1847 a secret society of such workers, using the ominous name "Communist League," commissioned Marx and Engels to write a programmatic statement. Seizing the occasion, Marx condensed his new theory into shock phrases as a revolutionary catechism. The result was that marvelously timed masterpiece of propagandistic literature which was the *Manifesto* of 1848.

The *Manifesto*'s aim was to promote a Second Coming of the French Revolution in socialist guise, an aim common to a range of radical sects of the 1840s. The route to their ambition ran as follows.

The revolution of 1789–93 had for the first time in history posed the question of "democracy" in its modern sense—that is, a polity founded on the proposition that all men, simply by virtue of being human, are equal before the law and endowed with full rights of participation in government. These principles are summed up as "the rights of man and the citizen" and "universal suffrage." The events of 1789 did not, of course, succeed in institutionalizing universal (manhood) suffrage democracy; but this is not to say it "failed," as is often averred. It had accomplished the epochal feat of mortally wounding Europe's millennial *ancien régime,* thus putting egalitarian democracy at the heart of the agenda of modernity.

After two centuries of modernity, it is difficult to

grasp the full "otherness" of the Old Regime. It was a world where all authority came from above, from God and/or nature; and where society was legally divided into unequal, hereditary "orders" or "estates" and, economically, into closed craft guilds. Modern democracy was born by inverting this sacred, corporate order, thereby making the people "sovereign" in place of the former absolute monarch. And once this had been accomplished in the largest state of Europe, the Old Regime was menaced everywhere else.

At the same time, the dynamic unleashed by 1789 threatened its proudest accomplishment: the liberal individualism enshrined in its new civic rights. For replacing the society of "orders" by one of citizens had not made men equal in fact. Rather, it had laid bare a new hierarchy founded on differences of wealth, an inequality all the more invidious since it was cloaked in nominal equality. This first became apparent when, following the defeat of the Jacobins' democratic Republic by the "Thermidorian reaction" of 1794, the "Conspiracy of the Equals" of Gracchus Babeuf schemed to establish a leveling dictatorship of the dispossessed. (Marx probably took the title "Manifesto" from their programmatic statement of 1796.)

The real turn towards a radicalism beyond liberal individualism, however, was the Paris Revolution of July 1830. This workers' revolt was immediately captured by the upper classes who established the "bourgeois monarchy" of Louis-Philippe, with a property suffrage enfranchising no more than a fraction of the population. It was now quite painfully clear to the "people" that equality before the law did not produce genuine, human equality; behind the "citizen" there in fact stood merely the "bourgeois." True human emancipation, consequently, could be achieved only through some measure of equalization of wealth—if necessary, forced.

Accordingly, the period 1830–48 became the seed-time of modern socialism. This movement was mostly devoted to producing social "harmony," not class struggle, as in the cooperative schemes of Robert Owen and Charles Fourier, the technocratic planning of Henri de Saint-Simon, the welfare state proposals of Louis Blanc, or the communitarian "communism" of Etienne Cabet—positions Marx and Engels branded "utopian." But there was a revolutionary socialism as well, as in the insurrectionary schemes of Auguste Blanqui, which harkened back to Babeuf and were also called "communist."

Moreover, 1789 had created the belief that revolutions are the way history happens—"the locomotives of history" in Marx's metaphor. And this belief was especially appealing to workers expelled from their guilds into the laissez-faire economy of the liberals. Thus, since 1830 had fallen pitifully short of democratic expectations, the Left now awaited a sequel—but on the higher level of a social 1789. Although such expectations were strongest in France, they were also widespread in the nascent English labor movement called Chartism, which sought to extend the Parliamentary franchise reform of 1832 all the way to universal suffrage—in effect, a revolution by legal means.

*   *   *

It was in this atmosphere of millenarian anticipation that Marx formulated his system. His point of departure, however, was not the "pauperism" spawned by the new industry (which as yet hardly existed in Germany), but the degrading spectacle of Germany's backwardness vis-à-vis France and England. And this lag he defined above all in political terms: Germany still lived in the "Middle Ages" under a monarchical and aristocratic Old Regime unchanged by the "partial emancipation" that France and England had achieved in 1830–32.

However, since the ante of modernity had now been upped from political democracy to socialism, Marx opined that Germany need not repeat 1789: she could telescope her bourgeois and socialist revolutions into a single "permanent revolution," as he called it in 1850. And he emphasized the centrality of this combined revolution to his system by concluding the *Manifesto* with the now odd-sounding claim that: "The Communists turn their attention chiefly to Germany." Thus, Marxism was born, not as a critique of mature capitalism, as is usually supposed, but as a theory of revolution to overcome German backwardness.

Such a revolution was possible, first, because France would fire up the socialist locomotive, and Germany could simply hitch onto it as it ran. Second, it was possible because Germany's very backwardness conferred on her one great advantage: the poverty of her real life had given her a superior capacity for philosophical understanding. Germany thus constituted the "theoretical consciousness" of what more advanced nations had already "done" in politics. This superiority would permit German socialists to give their impending revolution "conscious" direction to the highest goals of History.

But who would furnish the revolution's muscle? Marx's answer, of course, was the proletariat, but not because it was already an actor on the German scene. Rather, he established the proletariat's mission by theoretical deduction from his concept of freedom. This concept, however, had nothing to do with what John Stuart Mill or Alexis de Tocqueville understood by freedom—that is, freedom from external coercion. It was rather the freedom that Hegel equated with humanity's achievement, at the pinnacle of its development, of absolute "self-consciousness"—namely, full understanding of the laws of Reason in History.

When Marx first stood Hegel on his head, in *The German Ideology,* the formula came out as follows. The human condition is, first, one of "alienating" dependence on nature, which man invents tools to master. Technological development, however, leads to a "division of labor" which creates the further alienation of humanity split into warring social classes, thereby sundering the primal unity of the species. Marx's idea of "emancipation" from these dehumanizing forms of servitude, therefore, does not mean individual freedom. It means, rather, liberation of the species over the long haul of history from the socioeconomic shackles of its own creation.

The proletariat is the agent of this emancipation because it is the only class whose particular interest is synonymous with the general interests of humanity. And it is charged with this supreme mission precisely because it is the most exploited and hence most dehumanized class in existing society. As Marx put it on first mentioning the proletariat in 1843, it is the "universal class because its sufferings are universal." He thus defined the proletariat in the first instance not as the body of factory workers but as the metaphysical demiurge destined to liberate the species from social inequality: it was as the victim class that it became the redeemer class, the class to end all classes.

Marx's revolution would occur when the proletariat achieved "consciousness" of its dehumanized plight, and so also of its emancipatory mission. Thus this provincial German ideologue, freshly arrived in Paris, did not hesitate to proclaim: "*Philosophy* is the *head* of this emancipation and the *proletariat* is the *heart*." Thereby he made the proletariat the bearer of universal Reason; and his Communism became, not just equality, but the rational ordering of all human life.

And his dialectical logic rolled on: the social redemption of humanity would be produced by the very process of dependence that defined its historical Way of the Cross, for in Marx's appropriation of Hegel's para-Christian perspective, alienation is "self-enriching." The species therefore must suffer the degradations of ancient slavery, feudal serfdom, and bourgeois wage-labor exploitation to build the productive capacity to free itself not only from the blind forces of nature but also from the class divisions within the body social. Only thus would Man at last become his own master, exercising rational control over both his natural and his social environment.

And how, concretely, would mankind reach this ultimate state? Marx's answer was by destroying the false gods of liberal individualism: private property and the market. Yet at the same time he stood in never-ending awe of the technological miracles the bourgeoisie had wrought, as well as of its Promethean feat of organizing the world into a single market. Here, indeed, were elements of rationality that need only be appropriated by the proletariat to create the supreme rationality of Communism! The task of the impending proletarian revolution, therefore, was to liberate the wonder-working machine of modern industry from the fetters of bourgeois property relations.

Thus the Marxist synthesis is composed, basically, of two alluring components: On the one hand, there is the logic of history leading implacably to the point where the bourgeoisie "produces . . . its own gravediggers" in the form of the proletariat; and the struggle between the two classes is set forth dramatically in part I of the *Manifesto,* "Bourgeois and Proletarians," its most famous section and the only one read closely today. On the other hand, there is the revolutionary "consciousness" that the class struggle generates in the proletariat; and the Communist goals which that consciousness is expected to formulate are spelled out in part II, "Proletarians and Communists," a section now treated as secondary though it in fact points the way to Marxism's true historical destiny.

These goals are, first, to seize political power in order to "wrest, by degrees, all capital from the bourgeoisie," and then to "centralize all instruments of production in the hands of the State, i.e., of the proletariat organized as the ruling class." All production, moreover, would be "concentrated in the hands of the vast association of the whole nation" with "industrial armies, especially for agriculture," and a "common plan." In short, "the theory of Communism may be summed up in the single sentence: Abolition of private property." (Its additional, apparently moderate, goals, such as an income tax, were in fact also revolutionary at the time.) And what is vague in places of the *Manifesto* was clarified later in *Capital*, which offers one long excoriation of "commodity production for exchange" (i.e., manufacture for the market) and of the "bloodstained" medium of profit for "capital accumulation"—money. Marx's concrete program for "human emancipation," then, is nothing less than the abolition of private property, profit, the market, and indeed money.

And it is necessary to insist on this fact, for many commentators have refused to recognize it, holding that Marx, unlike "utopian" socialists, offered no vision of the future but only "scientific" knowledge of history's laws. The reason for this strange blindness, of course, is that once Stalin implemented that very program by mass violence many Westerners backed away from it, either preferring to believe that some other Bolshevik could have built a better socialism or choosing to read his doctrine only as a critique of capitalist society, as in the "Marxism without a proletariat" of the Frankfurt school.

In Marx himself, however, it is quite clear that "human emancipation" requires the absolute "negation" of private property, profit, and the market. Only once the victorious proletariat had implemented such full noncapitalism would society be liberated from both class inequality and state coercion. Only then would the world at last function "rationally," like one immense factory, and human labor would produce not capital, but the flowering of the species' hitherto alienated creative potential.

Yet there is a mystery at the heart of the *Manifesto*. It was issued in the name of a "party," and its proposals throughout are attributed to "The Communists." But who belongs to this "party"? The anonymous Communists claim they do not constitute a separate organization but have the same aims as "all other proletarian parties." In fact, the only definition given of the party is that it articulates "theoretical conclusions" which "merely express ... actual relations springing from an existing class struggle, from a historical movement going on under our very eyes." Hence it is ideological commitment, not social class, that defines the *Manifesto*'s "Communists." As of 1848, only Marx and Engels could qualify as members.

What Marx is saying, then, is that his theories are at once (a) the end product of the objective logic of history and (b) the voice of the proletariat's subjective revolutionary consciousness. Thus, although he always insisted that "the emancipation of the working classes must be conquered by the working classes themselves," he was equally adamant that his theories were what the proletariat would necessarily arrive at once they achieved full class consciousness. Marxism is thus a circular, self-verifying system—like Hegel's.

And this explains the demolition of all rival socialist ideologies in part III of the *Manifesto*, "Socialist and Communist Literature." Though these polemics are now usually discounted as mere relics, in fact they establish an abiding trait of Marxism. They constitute a rhetorical purge in defense of the *Manifesto* as the One True Teaching, a doctrine for the end of history.

II: THEORETICAL ELABORATIONS

The Specter's first foray into real politics failed dismally, of course. Not only did 1848 fail to produce a social 1789; it brought to power a modernized conservatism with Napoleon III in France and, eventually, Prince Otto von Bismarck in Prussia-Germany.

So in another propagandistic masterpiece, *The Eighteenth Brumaire of Louis Bonaparte,* Marx declared that in 1848 the scenario of revolution had been played backwards: instead of advancing from absolute monarchy to democracy, it had regressed from (allegedly) incipient socialism to dictatorship, thus repeating the "tragedy" of 1789 as "farce." He blamed this outcome on bourgeois repression, of course, but above all on the "idiocy of rural life"; for it was the rural "sack of potatoes," the peasant proprietors of the new universal suffrage Republic, that had elected Bonaparte President. In sum, Europe was "not yet ripe" for socialism. Nevertheless, Marx's faith was unshaken that there would be a triumphant "next time," when Bonaparte fell, for history was on the Revolution's side.

Meanwhile, however, Marx had no choice but to return to refining history's logic. Now an émigré in England, he retreated to the British Museum to mine parliamentary Blue Books for data towards the "critique of political economy" he had been contemplating since *The German Ideology*. This was to be the capstone of his system, the detailed analysis of the "internal contradictions" governing history's culminating stage, the "bourgeois mode of production." The result, in 1867, was the first volume of *Capital* tracing the dialectic operating "with the inexorability of a law of Nature" to seal the bourgeoisie's doom and thus produce Communism. Inevitably, the grim picture it painted of Europe's most industrial society suggested that the Communist revolution must occur first in some such setting.

Therewith did Marx offer the most deterministic face of his system. And Engels in his *Anti-Dühring of* 1877 (and in later glosses on Marx) gave their joint system a still more positivistic cast by defining it as "dialectical materialism" and promoting Marx as the "Darwin of social science." He even became, in a sense, *Capital*'s co-author by finishing its last two volumes from notes after his colleague's death. And it is Engels' "scientific socialism" that largely defined Marxism for both the Second and the Third Internationals.

A mythic counterpoint to this definition, however, was given by the last hurrah of worker revolutionary consciousness in the West: in 1870 the Franco-Prussian War at last toppled Bonaparte, and the next year the Paris Commune raised the Red Flag for the first time in history. Marx therefore hailed the insurrection as the first ever workers' government, a regime he elsewhere called "dictatorship of the proletariat" and which he defined in quasi-anarchist terms as direct democracy of the people in both government and economics. The Commune, however, was bloodily repressed by a new and enduring universal suffrage Republic; for it was no social revolution at all but the fortuitous result of war. Even so, the Commune made Marxism's political fortune: Europe had blamed it (quite undeservedly) on Marx's feeble and ephemeral International Working Men's Association, usually called the First International.

After 1871, however, the breakdown of bourgeois society that *Capital* predicted became increasingly unlikely. Contrary to Marx's expectations, therefore, the book's impact turned out to be inversely proportional to the level of capitalist development across Europe. It was translated first into Russian, in 1872, but published in the language of the country analyzed, English, only in 1888.

Capital's primary addressee, however, was Germany: as the preface informed her immature public, the English case "showed them their future." This was true only to a point, however. After 1870 Imperial Germany was indeed on her way to becoming Europe's industrial giant; yet at the same time she remained an Old Regime by half, for Bismarck had stolen away the German revolution from Marx by uniting the country under Prussia's semi-autocracy.

The result was a paradox in Marxist terms. To be sure, after Marx's death in 1883 his message was at last the dominant one in German socialism. Yet this was due less to the effect of the new industrial "base" on the workers' consciousness than to that of the Imperial "superstructure" on socialism's intellectual leaders. Bismarck, by outlawing the Socialist party from 1878 to 1890, had insured that these leaders would remain "red." Indeed, since Germany's liberals largely supported the system that had brought them national glory, her socialists henceforth functioned both as the party of the workers and the party of democratic dissent from the Empire.

Even more paradoxical was Marx's precocious success in Russia. To be sure, the Russian revolutionaries of the day—peasant-oriented socialists called "populists"—quite misread him. They interpreted his depiction of the horrors of capitalism as a warning to Russia to avoid it at all costs, and so to jump directly from "feudalism" to socialism. They believed, moreover, that the collective land holding of Russia's peasant communes would permit such historical leapfrog. What is even more unscientific, when the peasants failed to rise up in response to the populists' appeals, these student intellectuals resorted to a Blanquist conspiracy, the People's Will, to destroy Tsarism by terror. And in 1881 they assassinated Emperor Alexander II—"illogical" perhaps, but indubitably revolutionary.

Marx was therefore sufficiently impressed to subscribe, at least partially, to their cause—the only prospect, after the Paris Commune's failure, of igniting his European Revolution. Indeed, the year before his death, in the preface to a Russian translation of the *Manifesto,* he watered down his logic so far as to allow that: "If the Russian Revolution becomes the signal for a proletarian revolution in the West, so that both complement each other, the present Russian common ownership of land may serve as the starting point of a communist development."

Thus did the dying Marx return to a variant of his scenario of 1848 for combined revolution in Germany. By the same token he unwittingly adumbrated Lenin's and Trotsky's actual strategy of 1917 for permanent revolution in Russia.

In short, Marxism, born as a theory to overcome historical retardation, continued to have its chief impact in Europe's laggard parts—Germany, Austria-Hungary, Poland, and Russia—where the central problem was less the evils of capitalism than the persisting power of the

Old Regime. Throughout this zone, moreover, Marxism's great names continued to be intellectuals: Karl Kautsky, Eduard Bernstein, Rosa Luxemburg, Georgii Plekhanov, rather than occasional ex-workers such as August Bebel.

It was with this generation that the *Manifesto* arrived at its fiftieth anniversary—and Marx's Marxism at its moment of truth. Indeed, ever since the failure of 1848 a specter had been haunting his doctrine: what should its adherents do if capitalism's logic failed to generate worker revolutionary consciousness? At the *fin de siècle,* history forced an answer. Industrialism had now spread as far east as Russia; and an (apparently) strong Second International embraced all national parties. It would thus seem only logical for revolutionary consciousness to flare up among the proletariat. But nary a spark appeared. And so the ground was prepared for Marxism's eventual split between reformist Social Democracy and revolutionary Communism—as well as for the unending debate over which of the two was the "true" heir.

On the one hand, by Engels' death in 1895, the largest workers' party in Europe, German Social Democracy, had become officially Marxist; and its Erfurt Program of 1891 had espoused the basic tenets of the *Manifesto* (minus explicit approval of violence). In the ensuing years, however, Germany's modest constitutionalism made the party legalistic and parliamentary in practice. So its leaders, especially the trade-union chiefs, increasingly put short-term reforms ahead of Marx's revolutionary goals.

Then, in 1898 Eduard Bernstein dared speak the awful truth: contrary to Marx's laws, capitalism was not breaking down and the workers were not becoming revolutionary. The only conclusion for ethically committed socialists, therefore, was that their "movement meant everything" and the "final goal nothing."

In answer, on the Left Rosa Luxemburg sought to update Marx by substituting the mass strike for barricades. In the center, Karl Kautsky led the party's majority in condemning Bernstein's "revisionism" as a fundamental departure from Marx (which it indeed was). Yet at the same time, this reassertion of "orthodoxy" remained ambiguous. For Kautsky still anticipated that capitalism's logic would lead to Marx's propertyless, marketless Communism—though through electoral victory rather than street action. The SD's subsequent career, however, would reveal that this "evolutionary revolution" was as utopian in its way as Marx's big red bang.

Second International Marxism had a reverse fate when imported into Russia, where there was no semi-constitution or trade unions to provide the illusion of an evolution to Communism. At first, in the 1880s, Plekhanov, reacting against the populists' revolutionary romanticism, made Marx's logic more confining still by insisting that Russia would require two distinct revolutions to reach the Communist goal, one bourgeois and the other proletarian. Yet at the same time, this scenario accorded the workers "hegemony" even in the first revolution. Once revolution actually loomed, however, this lockstep orthodoxy proved to be unbearably convoluted and slow.

It is this dilemma that brought Lenin back from "orthodoxy" to the young Marx's "permanent revolution." He did so, however, with the notable corollary of a "party of a new type" to oversee its execution. For the revisionist crisis had convinced him that only such an instrument could liquidate the then half-century accumulated deficit of revolutionary worker consciousness. And so, in 1902, in *What Is to Be Done?* Lenin, then thirty-two, launched his theory of a vanguard of professional revolutionaries. Thus did this provincial Russian ideologue, freshly arrived in Munich to edit the journal of Russian Marxism, *Iskra* (*The Spark*), propose the winning remedy for rekindling the revolutionary flame. And thereby he at last gave organizational substance to the ideological "Communist party" defined in the *Manifesto*.

Lenin agreed, in effect, with Bernstein by insisting "that by its own resources alone the working class is in a position to generate only a trade-union consciousness." But he concluded from this fact that only a vanguard of professional revolutionaries could bring to the proletariat, "from without," the socialist "consciousness" which worker "spontaneity" was unable to generate on its own. For the "profound scientific knowledge" that produced socialism "was born in the heads" of Marxists drawn from the *"bourgeois intelligentsia"* (Lenin's emphasis).

Therewith Lenin substituted an intelligentsia party

for the proletariat. But only at such a price was it possible to put real muscle on the Specter.

III: PRACTICAL APPLICATIONS

Yet it was neither the logic of history nor proletarian class consciousness that put this "party of a new type" over the top. The brutal contingency of the First World War supplied the real impetus.

The War accomplished this, first, by discrediting the revolutionary credentials of Kautsky's orthodox Social Democrats. Its outbreak conclusively demonstrated that they were merely reformist, and, at that, only within the bounds of patriotism. And its conclusion, with Germany's defeat, at last brought these "Marxists" to power in the Weimar Republic, though now under the trade union leader and party bureaucrat Friedrich Ebert, who was hardly even reformist. All the same, the Social Democrats continued to insist that their movement was the sole orthodox one—even though it now suspiciously resembled what Marx had always excoriated as "petty bourgeois democracy."

In Russia, by contrast, war put revolutionary Marxists in power. Once military reverses and economic privation had toppled Tsarism in February 1917, Russian workers "spontaneously" formed grassroots "soviets," or councils, as organs of class power; and Lenin, in *State and Revolution,* hailed them as a rebirth of the direct democracy of the Paris Commune. Spurning the caution of the Mensheviks (still faithful to Plekhanov's two-stage revolution), he called for "all power to the soviets"—bodies, he held, that offered the base for a new "dictatorship of the proletariat." And so, using the anarchic social implosion of 1917 as a springboard, the Bolsheviks seized power in an October coup d'état soon heard round the world. By doing so, they also staked their claim to be the vanguard "consciousness" of the world proletariat. They saw their gamble as the beginning of a combined revolution with all of advanced Europe, which would then come to backward Russia's aid.

But it soon turned out that the soviets were no more than permanent mass meetings incapable of governing anything. In 1918, therefore, when these councils began to veer back to the Mensheviks, the Bolsheviks reduced them to the status of an administrative apparatus for what was now a plain party dictatorship. And of course, by 1920 the European revolution had failed to materialize, thus condemning the Soviet party-state to isolation in an overwhelmingly peasant country.

Accordingly, Kautsky and the Mensheviks proclaimed that Lenin's Marxism was merely a cloak for his reversion to the specifically Russian, and minoritarian, methods of The People's Will; and most Western commentators since have agreed with them. Elite revolutionism, however, is hardly specifically Russian. As other epithets then applied to Lenin indicate, he was in the quite European tradition of the Jacobins, or more exactly, of Babeuf—the models also, be it noted, of The People's Will.

Moreover, Lenin's chief amendment to Marxism— "the vanguard party"—finds good intellectual warrant in the Founder himself. To be sure, Marx never formed an organization comparable to the Leninist party. Yet he did furnish the theoretical basis for such a body by asserting in the *Manifesto* that the Communists (i.e., himself and Engels) "have over the great mass of the proletariat the advantage of clearly understanding the line of march, the conditions, and the ultimate general results of the proletarian movement." This statement attests, further, that on a more general level there exists a deep connection between Marx's idea of Communism as conscious, rational mastery over mankind's collective fate and Lenin's idea of the Party as the controlling vanguard of the spontaneous mass movement.

In this latter capacity Marxism continued to guide Bolshevik policy once the "proletarian" Party found itself isolated in a peasant country. To survive in an increasingly hostile society, the Party thus fell back on Marx's cult of industrial rationality in conjunction with his principle of class struggle. The outcome was the War Communism of 1918–21: private property, profit, the market, and indeed money were abolished (at least on paper); and "class warfare" was carried to the villages to extort food from peasant "kulaks." Full Communism, the Party declared, was at hand. In fact, economic collapse and famine ensued.

This outcome, however, cannot be attributed to an over-response to the civil war emergency, as the defeated Bolsheviks later claimed and as many Western historians have uncritically continued to repeat. War Communism, rather, was a grandiose social experiment, a fact which Nikolai Bukharin made clear at the time in his messianic *The ABC of Communism*. Moreover, as he later explained, since the Bolsheviks believed their revolution might well fail, they attempted an immediate leap to Communism to leave a glorious example for the future, as the Paris Commune had.

To be sure, once disaster forced the Party to revert to a mixed economy with the New Economic Policy (NEP) of 1921, Bukharin argued that the market was the most expedient way "to grow into socialism." Nonetheless, his goal remained Marx's full noncapitalism, not "market socialism" as some Sovietologists would have it. Yet as the NEP unfolded, the market power of the peasants increasingly threatened the political power of the Party.

So it fell to Stalin, in 1929–34, to execute the definitive leap to utopia with his "great offensive" to finally "build socialism." In winning this victory, however, he fully revealed the perverse logic of Marxism as an ideology for surmounting backwardness. Marx, after all, had supposed that the bourgeoisie would do all the hard work to make his vision possible. Yet a caprice of historical logic had brought his theories to power for the first time in the backward East rather than the advanced West, thus compelling the Russian "proletariat" to undertake the bourgeoisie's dirty business in its place—by coercion and from above. The Party therefore turned Marxism's other basic component, the class struggle, against the "petty bourgeois" peasants to create "industrial armies in agriculture," or *kolkhozes*. And with this "socialist primitive accumulation of capital" the Party-state financed its "planned" industrialization.

Thus was Marx's abolition of "commodity production for exchange" translated into enduring institutions. And so, under Stalin, the superstructure of the Leninist Party at last created the industrial and proletarian base that was supposed to have created *it*.

Of course, Stalin's "plans" were not genuine plans, since the total control of economic life to which they aspired is impossible. They represented little more than military methods in the service of crash economic development. Nonetheless, Marxism was the sine qua non of their success; for the mystique of Communism as the "scientific" control of reality was indispensable to legitimize, and to camouflage, their violence and waste.

Nor was such a "total" program driven by atavistic Russian nationalism, as is often alleged. The Party meticulously justified its every action with Marxist categories (however strained), and strove to create a "new socialist man" through ceaseless "agit-prop." Indeed the Leader in person—no mere power-hungry cynic as is also often alleged—wrote the chapter on dialectical materialism for the Party breviary, the *Short Course* of

1938. Thus did Stalin's regime attain the Orwellian acme of Communism as totalitarianism.

And a decade later it looked as though this total system might well triumph worldwide. In 1949—as if to celebrate the centennial of the *Manifesto*—Mao Zedong led a peasant army to plant the Red Flag in Beijing; and for twenty-five years he proceeded to emulate Stalin, indeed often surpassing him in radical delirium. At the same time, Stalin's more subdued successor, Nikita Khrushchev, boasted that by 1980 Soviet Russia would overtake the United States economically. Indeed, so fearsome did the global Communist tide appear that as late as the 1970s the CIA was still telling Washington that the Soviet GNP was sixty percent of its own (twenty percent would be closer to the truth).

Then, in 1989, it abruptly became clear that the Specter was just that—a phantom and an illusion. By 1939 Stalin's "command economy" had worked well enough to build a 1929 industrial plant; and against the background of the Great Depression this had appeared a major feat. This plant then proved sufficient to bring the country victoriously through the Second World War; and, with the addition of some higher technology, indeed to eventual nuclear parity with the United States in the Cold War. After the 1960s, however, the system turned out to be incapable of advancing from raw, extensive development to its sophisticated, intensive sequel. And by 1980 it was becoming clear, even to the Kremlin, that a regime of Party, Plan, and Police cannot outproduce a society of private property, profit, and the market.

The whole point of Communism, however, had been to outdo and supersede "capitalism." So Mikhail Gorbachev administered an elixir of *perestroika* and *glasnost* to rejuvenate the Soviet system without reneging on "the national choice made in October." The potion proved lethal, however. For revealing even a modicum of truth about "really-existing socialism" (in Leonid Brezhnev's formulation) only demonstrated that victory in the "international class struggle" had long since gone to the other side.

The Marxist mystique holding the system together was therefore discredited unto death; and the whole jerry-built structure collapsed almost overnight. For there were no longer any ideological class warriors to defend it. There remained only a Party *nomenklatura* content to settle for privatizing the rubble.

IV: OBITUARY FOR A SPENT SPECTER

So why did Marx's project for "human emancipation" lead in practice first to terror, and then to abject failure? The question is, indeed, a burning one because of the huge capital of hope Marx's system had accumulated over a century and a half. For his theory offered the winning modern answer to a longing for Utopia as old as Plato's *Republic*. It proposed the perfect society—just, fraternal, rational (and now industrial)—and made its advent seem not utopian at all but scientifically inevitable, even imminent.

To accept its failure as definitive, therefore, would be, for many, to mock the human sufferings it sought to redeem. Accordingly, the project's sad outcome has often been explained by de-coupling Marx from his proclaimed heirs: Lenin betrayed Marx, or Stalin betrayed both Marx and Lenin (into the bargain cutting short the Trotsky and/ or Bukharin "alternatives"). But this litany of bad luck runs on too long to pass as the credible cause of a failure so monumental. Hence the autopsy usually shades off into a broader thesis: backward, peasant Russia was "not yet ripe" for socialism. But is this not simply a variation on Marx's own wishful thoughts after the "farcical" failure of 1848? The real explanation, therefore, must be that there has never been a society—anywhere, anytime— that was "ripe" for what the *Manifesto* proposed.

And indeed, a hundred and fifty years of empirical history ought to make clear that the Communist failure stems from the perverse logic of Marx's project itself. For the two main axes of his theory—historical necessity and revolutionary worker consciousness—have never intersected in mundane reality. Not illogically, therefore, Marxism in practice produced the opposite of the results intended in theory, for only force could close the gap.

On the one hand (as a disabused Bernstein saw a century ago) the "logic" of industrial society does not lead to Communism; it leads to a prosaic welfare-state—which is where the "orthodox" Kautsky wound up too. And this outcome can only be welcomed. But Marxism is hardly necessary to achieve it: Fabianism or a mere New Deal can do as much.

On the other hand (as the Soviet "experiment" revealed) "proletarian" revolution can be brought to society only by such professional bearers of revolutionary consciousness as hail "from the *bourgeois intelligentsia*." And they can do this only by waging "class war" against their putative social base.

For there is no such thing in history as a proletarian revolution (or a bourgeois one, either: 1789 is far better summed up as broadly "democratic" than as narrowly "bourgeois"). In fact, both class revolutions are eschatological myths pointing the way to a "radiant future" beyond human alienation. Nor is there any such thing as "socialist society" waiting at the exit from "capitalism"; there is only a Soviet-type regime. And it *is* necessary to be Marxist to gamble other people's sufferings on building such a surreally-existing Sovietism.

The result of this wager, however, is not "human emancipation"; it is bondage to an ideocratic party-state. Lenin, Stalin, and Mao Zedong did not betray Marx. Rather, their substitution of a Communist Party (however peasant its membership) for the philosophical proletariat of the *Manifesto* could alone bring Marx's Specter crashing into really-existing history.

—MARTIN MALIA

MANIFESTO
OF THE
COMMUNIST PARTY

PREFACE TO THE
GERMAN EDITION OF 1872

The Communist League, an international association of
workers, which could of course be only a secret one, under the conditions obtaining at the time, commissioned
us, the undersigned, at the Congress held in London
in November, 1847, to write for publication a detailed
theoretical and practical programme of the Party. Such
was the origin of the following *Manifesto*, the manuscript of which travelled to London to be printed a few
weeks before the February Revolution. First published
in German, it has been republished in that language in
at least twelve different editions in Germany, England
and America. It was published in English for the first
time in 1850 in the *Red Republican,* London, translated
by Miss Helen Macfarlane, and in 1871 in at least three
different translations in America. The French version
first appeared in Paris shortly before the June insurrection of 1848, and recently in *Le Socialiste* of New York.
A new translation is in the course of preparation. A Polish version appeared in London shortly after it was first
published in German. A Russian translation was published in Geneva in the 'sixties. Into Danish, too, it was
translated shortly after its first appearance.

However much the state of things may have altered

during the last twenty-five years, the general principles laid down in this *Manifesto* are, on the whole, as correct to-day as ever. Here and there some detail might be improved. The practical application of the principles will depend, as the *Manifesto* itself states, everywhere and at all times, on the historical conditions for the time being existing, and, for that reason, no special stress is laid on the revolutionary measures proposed at the end of Section II. That passage would, in many respects, be very differently worded to-day. In view of the gigantic strides of modern industry since 1848, and of the accompanying improved and extended organisation of the working class, in view of the practical experience gained, first in the February Revolution, and then, still more, in the Paris Commune, where the proletariat for the first time held political power for two whole months, this programme has in some details become antiquated. One thing especially was proved by the Commune, viz., that "the working class cannot simply lay hold of the ready-made state machinery, and wield it for its own purposes." (See *The Civil War in France; Address of the General Council of the International Working Men's Association,* 1871, where this point is further developed.) Further, it is self-evident that the criticism of socialist literature is deficient in relation to the present time, because it comes down only to 1847; also that the remarks on the relation of the Communists to the various opposition parties (Section IV), although in principle still correct, yet in practice are antiquated, because the political situation has been entirely changed, and the prog-

ress of history has swept from off the earth the greater
portion of the political parties there enumerated.

But then, the *Manifesto* has become a historical document which we have no longer any right to alter. A subsequent edition may perhaps appear with an introduction
bridging the gap from 1847 to the present day; but this
reprint was too unexpected to leave us time for that.

—KARL MARX. FREDERICK ENGELS
London, 24 June, 1872.

PREFACE TO THE
RUSSIAN EDITION OF 1882

The first Russian edition of the *Manifesto of the Communist Party,* translated by Bakunin, was published
early in the 'sixties by the printing office of the *Kolokol.*
Then the West could see in it (the Russian edition of the
Manifesto) only a literary curiosity. Such a view would
be impossible to-day.

What a limited field the proletarian movement occu-
pied at that time (December, 1847) is most clearly shown
by the last section: the position of the Communists in
relation to the various opposition parties in the various
countries. Precisely Russia and the United States are
missing here. It was the time when Russia constituted

the last great reserve of all European reaction, when the United States absorbed the surplus proletarian forces of Europe through immigration. Both countries provided Europe with raw materials and were at the same time markets for the sale of its industrial products. Both were therefore, in one way or another, pillars of the existing European system.

How very different to-day. Precisely European immigration fitted North America for a gigantic agricultural production, whose competition is shaking the very foundations of European landed property—large and small. At the same time it enabled the United States to exploit its tremendous industrial resources with an energy and on a scale that must shortly break the industrial monopoly of Western Europe, and especially of England, existing up to now. Both circumstances react in a revolutionary manner upon America itself. Step by step the small and middle land ownership of the farmers, the basis of the whole political constitution, is succumbing to the competition of giant farms; at the same time a mass industrial proletariat and a fabulous concentration of capital funds are developing for the first time in the industrial regions.

And now Russia! During the Revolution of 1848–49 not only the European princes, but the European bourgeois as well, found their only salvation from the proletariat just beginning to awaken in Russian intervention. The Tsar was proclaimed the chief of European reaction. To-day he is a prisoner of war of the revolution in Gatchina, and Russia forms the vanguard of revolutionary action in Europe.

The *Communist Manifesto* had as its object the proclamation of the inevitable impending dissolution of modern bourgeois property. But in Russia we find, face to face with the rapidly flowering capitalist swindle and bourgeois property, just beginning to develop, more than half the land owned in common by the peasants. Now the question is: can the Russian *obshchina,* though greatly undermined, yet a form of the primaeval common ownership of land, pass directly to the higher form of Communist common ownership? Or on the contrary, must it first pass through the same process of dissolution such as constitutes the historical evolution of the West?

The only answer to that possible to-day is this: If the Russian Revolution becomes the signal for a proletarian revolution in the West, so that both complement each other, the present Russian common ownership of land may serve as the starting point for a communist development.

— KARL MARX. FREDERICK ENGELS

London, 21 January, 1882.

PREFACE TO THE
GERMAN EDITION OF 1883

The preface to the present edition I must, alas, sign alone. Marx, the man to whom the whole working class of Europe and America owes more than to any one else—rests at Highgate cemetery and over his grave the first grass is already growing. Since his death, there can be even less thought of revising or supplementing the *Manifesto*. But I consider it all the more necessary again to state the following expressly:

The basic thought running through the *Manifesto*—that economic production and the structure of society of every historical epoch necessarily arising therefrom constitute the foundation for the political and intellectual history of that epoch; that consequently (ever since the dissolution of the primaeval communal ownership of land) all history has been a history of class struggles, of struggles between exploited and exploiting, between dominated and dominating classes at various stages of social evolution; that this struggle, however, has now reached a stage where the exploited and oppressed class (the proletariat) can no longer emancipate itself from the class which exploits and oppresses it (the bourgeoisie), without at the same time forever freeing the whole of society from exploitation, oppression and class struggles—this basic thought belongs solely and exclusively to Marx.*

---

*"This proposition," I wrote in the preface to the English translation, "which, in my opinion, is destined to do for history what Darwin's theory has done for biology, we, both of us, had been gradually approaching for some years before 1845. How far I had independently progressed towards it is best shown by my *Condition of the Working Class in England*. But when I again met Marx at Brussels, in spring, 1845, he had it already worked out, and put it before me, in terms almost as clear as those in which I have stated it here." [*Note by F. Engels.*]

I have already stated this many times; but precisely now is it necessary that it also stand in front of the *Manifesto* itself.

—FREDERICK ENGELS

London, 28 June, 1883.

PREFACE TO THE GERMAN EDITION OF 1890

Since the above was written, a new German edition of the *Manifesto* has again become necessary, and much has also happened to the *Manifesto* which should be recorded here.

A second Russian translation—by Vera Zasulich—appeared at Geneva in 1882; the preface to that edition was written by Marx and myself. Unfortunately, the original German manuscript has gone astray; I must therefore re-translate from the Russian which will in no way improve the text. It reads:

"The first Russian edition of the *Manifesto of the Communist Party,* in Bakunin's translation, was published early in the 'sixties by the printing offices of the *Kolokol.* At that date a Russian edition of the *Manifesto* had for the West the significance, at most, of a literary curiosity. To-day such a view is no longer possible. How limited the area of the spread of the proletarian movement was at the time the *Manifesto* was first published (January, 1848) is best shown by the last section, *The Position of the Communists in Relation to the Various Opposition Parties*. Russia and the United States above all are missing. It was the time when Russia constituted the last great reserve of European reaction and when emigration to the United States absorbed the surplus forces of the European proletariat. Both countries provided Europe with raw materials, and served at the same time as markets for the sale of its industrial products. Both appeared therefore, in one way or another, as pillars of the European social order.

"What a change has taken place since then! Precisely European emigration has made possible the gigantic growth of agriculture in North America, which through its competition is shaking the very foundations of great and small landed property in Europe. At the same time it enabled the United States to begin the exploitation of its abundant industrial resources, and with such energy and on such a scale that in a short time it must put an end to the industrial monopoly of Western Europe. These two circumstances react in turn upon America in a revolutionary sense. More and more the small and middle land ownership of the independent farmers, the basis of the whole political system of America, is succumbing to the competition of giant farms, while simultaneously a numerous proletariat is emerging for the first time in the industrial regions alongside a fabulous concentration of capital.

"Let us now turn to Russia. At the time of the Revolution of 1848–49, not only the European monarchs, but the European bourgeois as well, looked upon Russian intervention as the only salvation from the proletariat, then for the first time becoming aware of its own strength. The Tsar was acclaimed the leader of European reaction. To-day he sits in Gatchina, a prisoner of war of the revolution, and Russia forms the vanguard of the revolutionary movement in Europe.

"The object of the *Communist Manifesto* was to proclaim the inevitable impending downfall of present-day bourgeois property. But in Russia we find—side by side with the feverishly growing capitalist system and the bourgeois land ownership just beginning to take shape—more than half the land owned in common by the peasant.

"Now the question is: can the Russian peasant community, this form of primaeval common ownership of land, although already very much disintegrated, pass directly to a higher communist form of land ownership or must it first pass through the same process of dissolution represented in the historical evolution of the West?

"The only answer to this question possible to-day is the following. If the Russian Revolution becomes the signal for a workers' revolution in the West, so that both complement each other, the present Russian common ownership of land may then serve as the starting point for a communist development.

"London, 21 January 1882."

At about the same date, a new Polish version appeared in Geneva: *Manifest Kommunistyczny*.

Furthermore, a new Danish translation has appeared in the *Socialdemokratisk Bibliothek,* Copenhagen, 1885. Unfortunately it is not quite complete; certain essential passages, which seem to have presented difficulties to the translator, have been omitted and in addition there are signs of carelessness here and there, which are all the more unpleasantly conspicuous since the translation indicates that had the translator taken a little more pains he would have done an excellent piece of work.

A new French version appeared in 1886 in *Le Socialiste* of Paris; it is the best published to date.

From this latter a Spanish version was published the same year in *El Socialista* of Madrid, and then reissued in pamphlet form: *Manifesto del Partido Communista* por Carlos Marx y F. Engels, Madrid, Administracion de El Socialista, Hernan Cortes 8.

As a matter of curiosity I may mention that in 1887 the manuscript of an Armenian translation was offered to a publisher in Constantinople. But the good man did not have the courage to publish something bearing the name of Marx and suggested that the translator set down his own name as author, which the latter however declined.

After one and then another of the more or less inaccurate American translations had been repeatedly reprinted in England, an authentic version at last appeared in 1888. This was by my friend Samuel Moore and we went through it together once more before it was sent to press. It is entitled: *Manifesto of the Communist Party,* by Karl Marx and Frederick Engels. Authorised

English translation, edited and annotated by Frederick Engels, 1888, London, William Reeves, 185 Fleet Street, E.C. I have added some of the notes of that edition to the present one.

The *Manifesto* has had a history of its own. Greeted with enthusiasm, at the time of its appearance, by the not at all numerous vanguard of scientific socialism (as is proved by the translations mentioned in the first preface), it was soon forced into the background by the reaction that began with the defeat of the Paris workers in June, 1848, and was finally excommunicated "by law" in the conviction of the Cologne Communists in November, 1852. With the disappearance from the public scene of the workers' movement that had begun with the February Revolution, the *Manifesto* too passed into the background.

When the European workers had again gathered sufficient strength for a new onslaught upon the power of the ruling classes, the International Working Men's Association came into being. Its aim was to weld together into *one* huge army the whole militant working class of Europe and America. Therefore it could not *set out* from the principles laid down in the *Manifesto*. It was bound to have a programme which would not shut the door on the English trade unions, the French, Belgian, Italian, and Spanish Proudhonists and the German Lassalleans. This programme—the considerations underlying the Statutes of the International—was drawn up by Marx with a master hand acknowledged even by Bakunin and the anarchists. For the ultimate final triumph of the ideas set forth in the *Manifesto,* Marx relied solely upon the intellectual development of the working class, as it necessarily had to ensue from united action and discussion. The events and vicissitudes in the struggle against capital, the defeats even more than the successes, could not but demonstrate to the fighters the inadequacy of their former universal panaceas and make their minds more receptive to a thorough understanding of the true conditions for working-class emancipation. And Marx was right. The working class of 1874, at the dissolution of the International, was altogether different from that of 1864, at its foundation. Proudhonism in the Latin countries and the specific Lassalleanism in Germany were dying out, and even the then arch-conservative English trade unions were gradually approaching the point where in 1887 the chairman of their Swansea Congress could say in their name: "Continental socialism has lost its terrors for us." Yet by 1887 continental socialism was almost exclusively the theory heralded in the *Manifesto*. Thus, to a certain extent, the history of the *Manifesto* reflects the history of the modern working-class movement since 1848. At present it is doubtless the most widely circulated, the most international product of all socialist literature, the common programme of many millions of workers of all countries from Siberia to California.

Nevertheless, when it appeared we could not have called it a *socialist* manifesto. In 1847 two kinds of people were considered socialists. On one hand were the adherents of the various utopian systems, notably the Owenites in England and the Fourierists in France, both of whom at that date had already dwindled to mere sects gradually dying out. On the other, the manifold types of social quacks who wanted to eliminate social abuses through their various universal panaceas and all kinds of patch-work, without hurting capital and profit in the least. In both cases, people who stood outside the labour movement and who looked for support rather to the "educated" classes. The section of the working class, however, which demanded a radical reconstruction of society, convinced that mere political revolutions were not enough, then called itself *Communist*. It was still a rough-hewn, only instinctive and frequently somewhat crude communism. Yet it was powerful enough to bring into being two systems of utopian communism—in France the "Icarian" communism of Cabet, and in Germany that of Weitling. Socialism in 1847 signified a bourgeois movement, communism a working-class movement. Socialism was, on the Continent at least, quite respectable, whereas communism was the very opposite. And since we were very decidedly of the opinion as early as then that "the emancipation of the workers must be the task of the working class itself," we could have no hesitation as to which of the two names we should choose. Nor has it ever occurred to us to repudiate it.

"Working men of all countries, unite!" But few voices responded when we proclaimed these words to the world forty-two years ago, on the eve of the first Paris Revolution in which the proletariat came out with the demands of its own. On 28 September 1864, however, the proletarians of most of the Western European countries joined hands in the International Working Men's Association of glorious memory. True, the International itself lived only nine years. But that the eternal union of the proletarians of all countries created by it is still alive and lives stronger than ever, there is no better witness than this day. Because to-day, as I write these lines, the European and American proletariat is reviewing its fighting forces, mobilised for the first time, mobilised as *one* army, under *one* flag, for *one* immediate aim: the standard eight-hour working day to be established by legal enactment, as proclaimed by the Geneva Congress of the International in 1866, and again by the Paris Workers' Congress in 1889. And to-day's spectacle will open the eyes of the capitalists and landlords of all countries to the fact that to-day the proletarians of all countries are united indeed.

If only Marx were still by my side to see this with his own eyes!

—FREDERICK ENGELS

London, 1 May, 1890.

PREFACE TO THE
ENGLISH EDITION OF 1888

The *Manifesto* was published as the platform of the Communist League, a working-men's association, first exclusively German, later on international, and, under the political conditions of the Continent before 1848, unavoidably a secret society. At a Congress of the League, held in November, 1847, Marx and Engels were commissioned to prepare for publication a complete theoretical and practical party programme. Drawn up in German, in January, 1848, the manuscript was sent to the printer in London a few weeks before the French revolution of 24 February. A French translation was brought out in Paris shortly before the insurrection of June, 1848. The first English translation, by Miss Helen Macfarlane, appeared in George Julian Harney's *Red Republican,* London, 1850. A Danish and a Polish edition had also been published.

The defeat of the Parisian insurrection of June, 1848—the first great battle between proletariat and bourgeoisie—drove again into the background, for a time, the social and political aspirations of the European working class. Thenceforth, the struggle for supremacy was again, as it had been before the Revolution of February, solely between different sections of the propertied class; the working class was reduced to a fight for political elbow-room, and to the position of extreme wing of the middle-class Radicals. Wherever independent proletarian movements continued to show signs of life, they were ruthlessly hunted down. Thus the Prussian police hunted out the Central Board of the Communist League then located in Cologne. The members were arrested, and, after eighteen months' imprisonment, they were tried in October, 1852. This celebrated "Cologne Communist Trial" lasted from 4 October till 12 November; seven of the prisoners were sentenced to terms of imprisonment in a fortress, varying from three to six years. Immediately after the sentence the League was formally dissolved by the remaining members. As to the *Manifesto,* it seemed thenceforth to be doomed to oblivion.

When the European working class had recovered sufficient strength for another attack on the ruling classes, the International Working Men's Association sprang up. But this association, formed with the express aim of welding into one body the whole militant proletariat of Europe and America, could not at once proclaim the principles laid down in the *Manifesto*. The International was bound to have a programme broad enough to be acceptable to the English trade unions, to the followers of Proudhon in France, Belgium, Italy, and Spain, and to the Lassalleans* in Germany. Marx, who

---

*Lassalle personally, to us, always acknowledged himself to be a disciple of Marx, and, as such, stood on the ground of the *Manifesto*. But in his public agitation, 1862–64, he did not go beyond demanding co-operative workshops supported by state credit. [*Note by F. Engels.*]

drew up this programme to the satisfaction of all parties, entirely trusted to the intellectual development of the working class, which was sure to result from combined action and mutual discussion. The very events and vicissitudes of the struggle against capital, the defeats even more than the victories, could not help bringing home to men's minds the insufficiency of their various favourite nostrums, and preparing the way for a more complete insight into the true conditions of working-class emancipation. And Marx was right. The International, on its breaking up in 1874, left the workers quite different men from what it had found them in 1864. Proudhonism in France, Lassalleanism in Germany were dying out, and even the conservative English trade unions, though most of them had long since severed their connection with the International, were gradually advancing towards that point at which, last year at Swansea, their president could say in their name: "Continental socialism has lost its terrors for us." In fact, the principles of the *Manifesto* had made considerable headway among the working men of all countries.

The *Manifesto* itself thus came to the front again. Since 1850 the German text had been reprinted several times in Switzerland, England, and America. In 1872 it was translated into English in New York, where the translation was published in *Woodhull and Claflin's Weekly*. From this English version a French one was made in *Le Socialiste* of New York. Since then at least two more English translations, more or less mutilated, have been brought out in America, and one of them has been reprinted in England. The first Russian translation, made by Bakunin, was published at Herzen's *Kolokol* office in Geneva, about 1863; a second one, by the heroic Vera Zasulich, also in Geneva, in 1882. A new Danish edition is to be found in *Socialdemokratisk Bibliothek,* Copenhagen, 1885; a fresh French translation in *Le Socialiste,* Paris, 1886. From this latter, a Spanish version was prepared and published in Madrid, in 1886. The German reprints are not to be counted; there have been twelve altogether at the least. An Armenian translation, which was to be published in Constantinople some months ago, did not see the light, I am told, because the publisher was afraid of bringing out a book with the name of Marx on it, while the translator declined to call it his own production. Of further translations into other languages I have heard but have not seen. Thus the history of the *Manifesto* reflects, to great extent, the history of the modern working-class movement; at present it is undoubtedly the most wide spread, the most international production of all socialist literature, the common platform acknowledged by millions of working men from Siberia to California.

Yet, when it was written, we could not have called it a *socialist* manifesto. By Socialists, in 1847, were understood, on the one hand the adherents of the various Utopian systems: Owenites in England, Fourierists in France, both of them already reduced to the position of mere sects, and gradually dying out; on the other hand, the most multifarious social quacks, who by all manner of tinkering, professed to redress, without any danger to capital and profit, all sorts of social grievances, in both cases men outside the working-class movement, and looking rather to the "educated" classes for support. Whatever portion of the working class had become convinced of the insufficiency of mere political revolutions, and had proclaimed the necessity of a total social change, called itself Communist. It was a crude, rough-hewn, purely instinctive sort of communism; still it touched the cardinal point and was powerful enough amongst the working class to produce the Utopian communism of Cabet in France, and of Weitling in Germany. Thus, in 1847, socialism was a middle-class movement, communism a working-class movement. Socialism was, on the Continent at least, "respectable"; communism was the very opposite. And as our notion, from the very beginning, was that "the emancipation of the working class must be the act of the working class itself," there could be no doubt as to which of the two names we must take. Moreover, we have, ever since, been far from repudiating it.

The *Manifesto* being our joint production, I consider myself bound to state that the fundamental proposition which forms its nucleus belongs to Marx. That proposition is: That in every historical epoch, the prevailing mode of economic production and exchange, and the social organisation necessarily following from it, form the basis upon which is built up, and from which alone can be explained the political and intellectual history of that epoch; that consequently the whole history of mankind (since the dissolution of primitive tribal society, holding land in common ownership) has been a history of class struggles, contests between exploiting and exploited, ruling and oppressed classes; that the history of these class struggles forms a series of evolutions in which, nowadays, a stage has been reached where the exploited and oppressed class—the proletariat—cannot attain its emancipation from the sway of the exploiting and ruling class—the bourgeoisie—without, at the same time, and once and for all emancipating society at large from all exploitation, oppression, class distinction and class struggles.

This proposition, which, in my opinion, is destined to do for history what Darwin's theory has done for biology, we, both of us, had been gradually approaching for some years before 1845. How far I had independently progressed towards it, is best shown by my *Conditions of the Working Class in England*. But when I again met Marx at Brussels, in spring, 1845, he had it already worked out, and put it before me, in terms almost as clear as those in which I have stated it here.

From our joint preface to the German edition of 1872, I quote the following:

"However much the state of things may have altered during the last twenty-five years, the general principles laid down in this *Manifesto* are, on the whole, as correct to-day as ever. Here and there some detail might be improved. The practical application of the principles will depend, as the *Manifesto* itself states, everywhere and at all times, on the historical conditions for the time being existing, and, for that reason, no special stress is laid on the revolutionary measures proposed at the end of Section II. That passage would, in many respects, be very differently worded to-day. In view of the gigantic strides of modern industry since 1848, and of the accompanying improved and extended organisation of the working class, in view of the practical experience gained, first in the February Revolution, and then, still more, in the Paris Commune, where the proletariat for the first time held political power for two whole months, this programme has in some details become antiquated. One thing especially was proved by the Commune, viz., that 'the working class cannot simply lay hold of the ready-made state machinery, and wield it for its own purposes.' (See *The Civil War in France; Address of the General Council of the International Working Men's Association,* 1871, where this point is further developed.) Further, it is self-evident that the criticism of socialist literature is deficient in relation to the present time, because it comes down only to 1847; also, that the remarks on the relation of the Communists to the various opposition parties (Section IV), although in principle still correct, yet in practice are antiquated, because the political situation has been entirely changed, and the progress of history has swept from off the earth the greater portion of the political parties there enumerated.

"But then, the *Manifesto* has become a historical document which we have no longer any right to alter."

The present translation is by Mr. Samuel Moore, the translator of the greater portion of Marx's *Capital.* We have revised it in common, and I have added a few notes explanatory of historical allusions.

—FREDERICK ENGELS

London, 30 January, 1888.

MANIFESTO OF THE COMMUNIST PARTY

A spectre is haunting Europe—the spectre of communism. All the powers of old Europe have entered into a holy alliance to exorcise this spectre: Pope and Tsar, Metternich and Guizot, French Radicals and German police-spies.

Where is the party in opposition that has not been decried as communistic by its opponents in power? Where is the opposition that has not hurled back the branding reproach of communism, against the more advanced opposition parties, as well as against its reactionary adversaries?

Two things result from this fact:

I. Communism is already acknowledged by all European powers to be itself a power.

II. It is high time that Communists should openly, in the face of the whole world, publish their views, their aims, their tendencies, and meet this nursery tale of the spectre of communism with a manifesto of the party itself.

To this end, Communists of various nationalities have assembled in London and sketched the following manifesto, to be published in the English, French, German, Italian, Flemish and Danish languages.

I. BOURGEOIS
AND PROLETARIANS*

The history of all hitherto existing society† is the history of class struggles.

---

*By bourgeoisie is meant the class of modern capitalists, owners of the means of social production and employers of wage labour. By proletariat, the class of modern wage labourers who, having no means of production of their own, are reduced to selling their labour power in order to live. [*Note by F. Engels to the English edition of 1888.*]

†That is, all *written* history. In 1847 the pre-history of society, the social organisation existing previous to recorded history, was all but unknown. Since then Haxthausen [August von, 1792–1866] discovered common ownership of land in Russia, Maurer [Georg Ludwig von] proved it to be the social foundation from which all Teutonic races started in history, and, by and by, village communities were found to be, or to have been, the primitive form of society everywhere from India to Ireland. The inner organisation of this primitive communistic society was laid bare, in its typical form, by Morgan's [Lewis Henry, 1818–81] crowning discovery of the true nature of the *gens* and its relation to the *tribe*. With the dissolution of these primaeval communities, society begins to be differentiated into separate and finally antagonistic classes. I have attempted to retrace this process of dissolution in *Der Ursprung der Familie, des Privateigenthums und des Staats* [*The Origin of the Family, Private Property and the State*], second edition, Stuttgart, 1886. [*Note by F. Engels to the English edition of 1888.*]

Freeman and slave, patrician and plebeian, lord and serf, guild-master* and journeyman, in a word, oppressor and oppressed, stood in constant opposition to one another, carried on an uninterrupted, now hidden, now open fight, a fight that each time ended, either in a revolutionary reconstitution of society at large, or in the common ruin of the contending classes.

In the earlier epochs of history, we find almost everywhere a complicated arrangement of society into various orders, a manifold gradation of social rank. In ancient Rome we have patricians, knights, plebeians, slaves; in the Middle Ages, feudal lords, vassals, guild-masters, journeymen, apprentices, serfs; in almost all of these classes, again, subordinate gradations.

The modern bourgeois society that has sprouted from the ruins of feudal society has not done away with class antagonisms. It has but established new classes, new conditions of oppression, new forms of struggle in place of the old ones.

Our epoch, the epoch of the bourgeoisie, possesses, however, this distinctive feature: It has simplified the class antagonisms. Society as a whole is more and more splitting up into two great hostile camps, into two great classes directly facing each other—bourgeoisie and proletariat.

From the serfs of the Middle Ages sprang the chartered burghers of the earliest towns. From these

*Guild-master, that is a full member of a guild, a master within, not a head of a guild. [*Note by F. Engels to the English edition of* 1888.]

burgesses the first elements of the bourgeoisie were developed.

The discovery of America, the rounding of the Cape, opened up fresh ground for the rising bourgeoisie. The East-Indian and Chinese markets, the colonisation of America, trade with the colonies, the increase in the means of exchange and in commodities generally, gave to commerce, to navigation, to industry, an impulse never before known, and thereby, to the revolutionary element in the tottering feudal society, a rapid development.

The feudal system of industry, in which industrial production was monopolised by closed guilds, now no longer sufficed for the growing wants of the new markets. The manufacturing system took its place. The guildmasters were pushed aside by the manufacturing middle class; division of labour between the different corporate guilds vanished in the face of division of labour in each single workshop.

Meantime the markets kept ever growing, the demand ever rising. Even manufacture no longer sufficed. Thereupon, steam and machinery revolutionised industrial production. The place of manufacture was taken by the giant, modern industry, the place of the industrial middle class by industrial millionaires, the leaders of whole industrial armies, the modern bourgeois.

Modern industry has established the world market, for which the discovery of America paved the way. This market has given an immense development to commerce, to navigation, to communication by land. This development has, in its turn, reacted on the extension of industry; and in proportion as industry, commerce, navigation, railways extended, in the same proportion the bourgeoisie developed, increased its capital, and pushed into the background every class handed down from the Middle Ages.

We see, therefore, how the modern bourgeoisie is itself the product of a long course of development, of a series of revolutions in the modes of production and of exchange.

Each step in the development of the bourgeoisie was accompanied by a corresponding political advance of that class. An oppressed class under the sway of the feudal nobility, an armed and self-governing association in the medieval commune;* here independent urban republic (as in Italy and Germany), there taxable "third estate" of the monarchy (as in France); afterwards, in the period of manufacture proper, serving either the semi-feudal or the absolute monarchy as a counterpoise against the nobility, and, in fact, cornerstone of the great monarchies in general—the bourgeoisie has at last, since the establishment of modern industry and of the

*This was the name given their urban communities by the townsmen of Italy and France, after they had purchased or conquered their initial rights of self-government from their feudal lords. [*Note by F. Engels to the German edition of* 1890.]

"Commune" was the name taken in France by the nascent towns even before they had conquered from their feudal lords and masters local self-government and political rights as the "Third Estate." Generally speaking, for the economical development of the bourgeoisie, England is here taken as the typical country, for its political development, France. [*Note by F. Engels to the English edition of* 1888.]

world market, conquered for itself, in the modern representative state, exclusive political sway. The executive of the modern state is but a committee for managing the common affairs of the whole bourgeoisie.

The bourgeoisie, historically, has played a most revolutionary part.

The bourgeoisie, wherever it has got the upper hand, has put an end to all feudal, patriarchal, idyllic relations. It has pitilessly torn asunder the motley feudal ties that bound man to his "natural superiors," and has left no other nexus between man and man than naked self-interest, than callous "cash payment." It has drowned the most heavenly ecstasies of religious fervour, of chivalrous enthusiasm, of philistine sentimentalism, in the icy water of egotistical calculation. It has resolved personal worth into exchange value, and in place of the numberless indefeasible chartered freedoms, has set up that single, unconscionable freedom—Free Trade. In one word, for exploitation, veiled by religious and political illusions, it has substituted naked, shameless, direct, brutal exploitation.

The bourgeoisie has stripped of its halo every occupation hitherto honoured and looked up to with reverent awe. It has converted the physician, the lawyer, the priest, the poet, the man of science, into its paid wage labourers.

The bourgeoisie has torn away from the family its sentimental veil, and has reduced the family relation to a mere money relation.

The bourgeoisie has disclosed how it came to pass

that the brutal display of vigour in the Middle Ages, which reactionaries so much admire, found its fitting complement in the most slothful indolence. It has been the first to show what man's activity can bring about. It has accomplished wonders far surpassing Egyptian pyramids, Roman aqueducts, and Gothic cathedrals; it has conducted expeditions that put in the shade all former exoduses of nations and crusades.

The bourgeoisie cannot exist without constantly revolutionising the instruments of production, and thereby the relations of production, and with them the whole relations of society. Conservation of the old modes of production in unaltered form, was, on the contrary, the first condition of existence for all earlier industrial classes. Constant revolutionising of production, uninterrupted disturbance of all social conditions, everlasting uncertainty and agitation distinguish the bourgeois epoch from all earlier ones. All fixed, fast frozen relations, with their train of ancient and venerable prejudices and opinions, are swept away, all new-formed ones become antiquated before they can ossify. All that is solid melts into air, all that is holy is profaned, and man is at last compelled to face with sober senses his real conditions of life and his relations with his kind.

The need of a constantly expanding market for its products chases the bourgeoisie over the whole surface of the globe. It must nestle everywhere, settle everywhere, establish connections everywhere.

The bourgeoisie has through its exploitation of the world market given a cosmopolitan character to production and consumption in every country. To the great chagrin of reactionaries, it has drawn from under the feet of industry the national ground on which it stood. All old-established national industries have been destroyed or are daily being destroyed. They are dislodged by new industries, whose introduction becomes a life and death question for all civilised nations, by industries that no longer work up indigenous raw material, but raw material drawn from the remotest zones; industries whose products are consumed, not only at home, but in every quarter of the globe. In place of the old wants, satisfied by the production of the country, we find new wants, requiring for their satisfaction the products of distant lands and climes. In place of the old local and national seclusion and self-sufficiency, we have intercourse in every direction, universal inter-dependence of nations. And as in material, so also in intellectual production. The intellectual creations of individual nations become common property. National one-sidedness and narrow-mindedness become more and more impossible, and from the numerous national and local literatures there arises a world literature.

The bourgeoisie, by the rapid improvement of all instruments of production, by the immensely facilitated means of communication, draws all, even the most barbarian, nations into civilisation. The cheap prices of its commodities are the heavy artillery with which it batters down all Chinese walls, with which it forces the barbarians' intensely obstinate hatred of foreigners to capitulate. It compels all nations, on pain of extinction, to adopt the bourgeois mode of production; it compels them to introduce what it calls civilisation into their midst, i.e., to become bourgeois themselves. In one word, it creates a world after its own image.

The bourgeoisie has subjected the country to the rule of the towns. It has created enormous cities, has greatly increased the urban population as compared with the rural, and has thus rescued a considerable part of the population from the idiocy of rural life. Just as it has made the country dependent on the towns, so it has made barbarian and semi-barbarian countries dependent on the civilised ones, nations of peasants on nations of bourgeois, the East on the West.

The bourgeoisie keeps more and more doing away with the scattered state of the population, of the means of production, and of property. It has agglomerated population, centralised means of production, and has concentrated property in a few hands. The necessary consequence of this was political centralisation. Independent, or but loosely connected provinces, with separate interests, laws, governments, and systems of taxation, became lumped together into one nation, with one government, one code of laws, one national class interest, one frontier and one customs tariff.

The bourgeoisie, during its rule of scarce one hundred years, has created more massive and more colossal productive forces than have all preceding generations together. Subjection of nature's forces to man, machinery, application of chemistry to industry and agriculture, steam navigation, railways, electric telegraphs, clearing of whole continents for cultivation, canalisation of rivers, whole populations conjured out of the ground—what earlier century had even a presentiment that such productive forces slumbered in the lap of social labour?

We see then: the means of production and of exchange, on whose foundation the bourgeoisie built itself up, were generated in feudal society. At a certain stage in the development of these means of production and of exchange, the conditions under which feudal society produced and exchanged, the feudal organisation of agriculture and manufacturing industry, in one word, the feudal relations of property became no longer compatible with the already developed productive forces; they became so many fetters. They had to be burst asunder; they were burst asunder.

Into their place stepped free competition, accompanied by a social and political constitution adapted to it, and by the economic and political sway of the bourgeois class.

A similar movement is going on before our own eyes. Modern bourgeois society with its relations of production, of exchange and of property, a society that has conjured up such gigantic means of production and of exchange, is like the sorcerer who is no longer able to control the powers of the nether world whom he has called up by his spells. For many a decade past the history of industry and commerce is but the history of the revolt of modern productive forces against modern conditions of production, against the property relations that are the conditions for the existence of the bourgeoisie and of its rule. It is enough to mention the commercial crises that by their periodical return put the existence of the entire bourgeois society on its trial, each time more threateningly. In these crises a great part not only of the existing products, but also of the previously created productive forces, are periodically destroyed. In these crises there breaks out an epidemic that, in all earlier epochs, would have seemed an absurdity—the epidemic of over-production. Society suddenly finds itself put back into a state of momentary barbarism; it appears as if a famine, a universal war of devastation had cut off the supply of every means of subsistence; industry and commerce seem to be destroyed. And why? Because there is too much civilisation, too much means of subsistence, too much industry, too much commerce. The productive forces at the disposal of society no longer tend to further the development of the conditions of bourgeois property; on the contrary, they have become too powerful for these conditions, by which they are fettered, and so soon as they overcome these fetters, they bring disorder into the whole of bourgeois society, endanger the existence of bourgeois property. The conditions of bourgeois society are too narrow to comprise the wealth created by them. And how does the bourgeoisie get over these crises? On the one hand, by enforced destruction of a mass of productive forces; on the other, by the conquest of new markets, and by the more thorough exploitation of the old ones. That is to say, by paving the way for more extensive and more destructive crises, and by diminishing the means whereby crises are prevented.

The weapons with which the bourgeoisie felled feudalism to the ground are now turned against the bourgeoisie itself.

But not only has the bourgeoisie forged the weapons that bring death to itself; it has also called into existence the men who are to wield those weapons—the modern working class—the proletarians.

In proportion as the bourgeoisie, i.e., capital, is developed, in the same proportion is the proletariat, the modern working class, developed—a class of labourers, who live only so long as they find work, and who find work only so long as their labour increases capital. These labourers, who must sell themselves piecemeal, are a commodity, like every other article of commerce, and are consequently exposed to all the vicissitudes of competition, to all the fluctuations of the market.

Owing to the extensive use of machinery and to division of labour, the work of the proletarians has lost all individual character, and, consequently, all charm for the workman. He becomes an appendage of the machine, and it is only the most simple, most monotonous, and most easily acquired knack, that is required of him. Hence, the cost of production of a workman is restricted, almost entirely, to the means of subsistence that he requires for his maintenance, and for the propagation of his race. But the price of a commodity, and therefore also of labour, is equal to its cost of production. In proportion, therefore, as the repulsiveness of the work increases, the wage decreases. Nay more, in proportion as the use of machinery and division of labour increases, in the same proportion the burden of toil also increases, whether by prolongation of the working hours, by increase of the work exacted in a given time, or by increased speed of the machinery, etc.

Modern industry has converted the little workshop of the patriarchal master into the great factory of the industrial capitalist. Masses of labourers, crowded into the factory, are organised like soldiers. As privates of the industrial army they are placed under the command of a perfect hierarchy of officers and sergeants. Not only are they slaves of the bourgeois class, and of the bourgeois state; they are daily and hourly enslaved by the machine, by the overlooker, and, above all, by the individual bourgeois manufacturer himself. The more openly this despotism proclaims gain to be its end and aim, the more petty, the more hateful and the more embittering it is.

The less the skill and exertion of strength implied in manual labour, in other words, the more modern industry becomes developed, the more is the labour of men superseded by that of women. Differences of age and sex have no longer any distinctive social validity for the working class. All are instruments of labour, more or less expensive to use, according to their age and sex.

No sooner is the exploitation of the labourer by the manufacturer, so far at an end, that he receives his wages in cash, than he is set upon by the other portions of the bourgeoisie, the landlord, the shopkeeper, the pawnbroker, etc.

The lower strata of the middle class—the small tradespeople, shopkeepers, and retired tradesmen generally,

the handicraftsmen and peasants—all these sink gradually into the proletariat, partly because their diminutive
capital does not suffice for the scale on which modern
industry is carried on, and is swamped in the competition with the large capitalists, partly because their spe-
cialised skill is rendered worthless by new methods of
production. Thus the proletariat is recruited from all
classes of the population.

The proletariat goes through various stages of development. With its birth begins its struggle with the bourgeoisie. At first the contest is carried on by individual
labourers, then by the work people of a factory, then by
the operatives of one trade, in one locality, against the
individual bourgeois who directly exploits them. They
direct their attacks not against the bourgeois conditions
of production, but against the instruments of production
themselves; they destroy imported wares that compete
with their labour, they smash to pieces machinery, they
set factories ablaze, they seek to restore by force the
vanished status of the workman of the Middle Ages.

At this stage the labourers still form an incoherent
mass scattered over the whole country, and broken up
by their mutual competition. If anywhere they unite to
form more compact bodies, this is not yet the consequence of their own active union, but of the union of
the bourgeoisie, which class, in order to attain its own
political ends, is compelled to set the whole proletariat
in motion, and is moreover yet, for a time, able to do
so. At this stage, therefore, the proletarians do not fight
their enemies, but the enemies of their enemies, the

remnants of absolute monarchy, the landowners, the non-industrial bourgeois, the petty bourgeoisie. Thus the whole historical movement is concentrated in the hands of the bourgeoisie; every victory so obtained is a victory for the bourgeoisie.

But with the development of industry the proletariat not only increases in number; it becomes concentrated in greater masses, its strength grows, and it feels that strength more. The various interests and conditions of life within the ranks of the proletariat are more and more equalised, in proportion as machinery obliterates all distinctions of labour, and nearly everywhere reduces wages to the same low level. The growing competition among the bourgeois, and the resulting commercial crises, make the wages of the workers ever more fluctuating. The unceasing improvement of machinery, ever more rapidly developing, makes their livelihood more and more precarious; the collisions between individual workmen and individual bourgeois take more and more the character of collisions between two classes. Thereupon the workers begin to form combinations (trade unions) against the bourgeois; they club together in order to keep up the rate of wages; they found permanent associations in order to make provision beforehand for these occasional revolts. Here and there the contest breaks out into riots.

Now and then the workers are victorious, but only for a time. The real fruit of their battles lies, not in the immediate result, but in the ever expanding union of the workers. This union is helped on by the improved means of communication that are created by modern industry, and that place the workers of different localities in contact with another. It was just this contact that was needed to centralise the numerous local struggles, all of the same character, into one national struggle between classes. But every class struggle is a political struggle. And that union, to attain which the burghers of the Middle Ages, with their miserable highways, required centuries, the modern proletarians, thanks to railways, achieve in a few years.

This organisation of the proletarians into a class, and consequently into a political party, is continually being upset again by the competition between the workers themselves. But it ever rises up again, stronger, firmer, mightier. It compels legislative recognition of particular interests of the workers, by taking advantage of the divisions among the bourgeoisie itself. Thus the Ten-Hours Bill in England was carried.

Altogether, collisions between the classes of the old society further in many ways the course of development of the proletariat. The bourgeoisie finds itself involved in a constant battle. At first with the aristocracy, later on, with those portions of the bourgeoisie itself, whose interests have become antagonistic to the progress of industry; at all time with the bourgeoisie of foreign countries. In all these battles it sees itself compelled to appeal to the proletariat, to ask for its help, and thus, to drag it into the political arena. The bourgeoisie itself, therefore, supplies the proletariat with its own elements of political and general education, in other words, it furnishes the proletariat with weapons for fighting the bourgeoisie.

Further, as we have already seen, entire sections of the ruling classes are, by the advance of industry, pre-cipitated into the proletariat, or are at least threatened in their conditions of existence. These also supply the proletariat with fresh elements of enlightenment and progress.

Finally, in times when the class struggle nears the de-cisive hour, the process of dissolution going on within the ruling class, in fact within the whole range of old society, assumes such a violent, glaring character, that a small section of the ruling class cuts itself adrift, and joins the revolutionary class, the class that holds the fu-ture in its hands. Just as, therefore, at an earlier period, a section of the nobility went over to the bourgeoisie, so now a portion of the bourgeoisie goes over to the proletariat, and in particular, a portion of the bourgeois ideologists, who have raised themselves to the level of comprehending theoretically the historical movement as a whole.

Of all the classes that stand face to face with the bourgeoisie to-day, the proletariat alone is a really revo-lutionary class. The other classes decay and finally disap-pear in the face of modern industry; the proletariat is its special and essential product.

The lower middle class, the small manufacturer, the shopkeeper, the artisan, the peasant, all these fight against the bourgeoisie, to save from extinction their ex-istence as fractions of the middle class. They are therefore not revolutionary, but conservative. Nay, more, they are reactionary, for they try to roll back the wheel of history. If by chance they are revolutionary, they are so only in view of their impending transfer into the proletariat; they thus defend not their present, but their future interests; they desert their own standpoint to place themselves at that of the proletariat.

The "dangerous class," the social scum, that passively rotting mass thrown off by the lowest layers of old society, may, here and there, be swept into the movement by a proletarian revolution; its conditions of life, however, prepare it far more for the part of a bribed tool of reactionary intrigue.

In the conditions of the proletariat, those of old society at large are already virtually swamped. The proletarian is without property; his relation to his wife and children has no longer anything in common with the bourgeois family relations; modern industrial labour, modern subjection to capital, the same in England as in France, in America as in Germany, has stripped him of every trace of national character. Law, morality, religion, are to him so many bourgeois prejudices, behind which lurk in ambush just as many bourgeois interests.

All the preceding classes that got the upper hand, sought to fortify their already acquired status by subjecting society at large to their conditions of appropriation. The proletarians cannot become masters of the productive forces of society, except by abolishing their own previous mode of appropriation, and thereby also every other previous mode of appropriation. They have nothing of their own to secure and to fortify; their mission is to destroy all previous securities for, and insurances of, individual property.

All previous historical movements were movements of minorities, or in the interest of minorities. The proletarian movement is the self-conscious, independent movement of the immense majority, in the interest of the immense majority. The proletariat, the lowest stratum of our present society, cannot stir, cannot raise itself up, without the whole superincumbent strata of official society being sprung into the air.

Though not in substance, yet in form, the struggle of the proletariat with the bourgeoisie is at first a national struggle. The proletariat of each country must, of course, first of all settle matters with its own bourgeoisie.

In depicting the most general phases of the development of the proletariat, we traced the more or less veiled civil war, raging within existing society, up to the point where that war breaks out into open revolution, and where the violent overthrow of the bourgeoisie lays the foundation for the sway of the proletariat.

Hitherto, every form of society has been based, as we have already seen, on the antagonism of oppressing and oppressed classes. But in order to oppress a class, certain conditions must be assured to it under which it can, at least, continue its slavish existence. The serf, in the period of serfdom, raised himself to membership in the commune, just as the petty bourgeois, under the yoke of feudal absolutism, managed to develop into a bourgeois. The modern labourer, on the contrary, instead of rising with the progress of industry, sinks deeper and deeper below the conditions of existence of his own class. He becomes a pauper, and pauperism develops more rapidly than population and wealth. And here it becomes evident that the bourgeoisie is unfit any longer to be the ruling class in society, and to impose its conditions of existence upon society as an overriding law. It is unfit to rule because it is incompetent to assure an existence to its slave within his slavery, because it cannot help letting him sink into such a state, that it has to feed him, instead of being fed by him. Society can no longer live under this bourgeoisie, in other words, its existence is no longer compatible with society.

The essential condition for the existence and for the sway of the bourgeois class, is the formation and augmentation of capital; the condition for capital is wage labour. Wage labour rests exclusively on competition between the labourers. The advance of industry, whose involuntary promoter is the bourgeoisie, replaces the isolation of the labourers, due to competition, by their revolutionary combination, due to association. The development of modern industry, therefore, cuts from under its feet the very foundation on which the bourgeoisie produces and appropriates products. What the bourgeoisie therefore produces, above all, are its own grave-diggers. Its fall and the victory of the proletariat are equally inevitable.

II. PROLETARIANS
AND COMMUNISTS

In what relation do the Communists stand to the proletarians as a whole?

The Communists do not form a separate party opposed to other working-class parties.

They have no interests separate and apart from those of the proletariat as a whole.

They do not set up any sectarian principles of their own, by which to shape and mold the proletarian movement.

The Communists are distinguished from the other working-class parties by this only: (1) In the national struggles of the proletarians of the different countries, they point out and bring to the front the common interests of the entire proletariat, independently of all nationality. (2) In the various stages of development which the struggle of the working class against the bourgeoisie has to pass through, they always and everywhere represent the interests of the movement as a whole.

The Communists, therefore, are on the one hand, practically, the most advanced and resolute section of the working-class parties of every country, that section which pushes forward all others; on the other hand, theoretically, they have over the great mass of the proletariat the advantage of clearly understanding the lines of march, the conditions, and the ultimate general results of the proletarian movement.

The immediate aim of the Communists is the same as that of all other proletarian parties: Formation of the proletariat into a class, overthrow of the bourgeois supremacy, conquest of political power by the proletariat.

The theoretical conclusions of the Communists are in no way based on ideas or principles that have been invented, or discovered, by this or that would-be universal reformer.

They merely express, in general terms, actual relations springing from an existing class struggle, from a historical movement going on under our very eyes. The abolition of existing property relations is not at all a distinctive feature of communism.

All property relations in the past have continually been subject to historical change consequent upon the change in historical conditions.

The French Revolution, for example, abolished feudal property in favour of bourgeois property.

The distinguishing feature of communism is not the abolition of property generally, but the abolition of bourgeois property. But modern bourgeois private property is the final and most complete expression of the system of producing and appropriating products that is based on class antagonisms, on the exploitation of the many by the few.

In this sense, the theory of the Communists may be summed up in the single sentence: Abolition of private property.

We Communists have been reproached with the desire of abolishing the right of personally acquiring property as the fruit of a man's own labour, which property is alleged to be the groundwork of all personal freedom, activity and independence.

Hard-won, self-acquired, self-earned property! Do you mean the property of the petty artisan and of the small peasant, a form of property that preceded the bourgeois form? There is no need to abolish that; the development of industry has to a great extent already destroyed it, and is still destroying it daily.

Or do you mean modern bourgeois private property?

But does wage labour create any property for the labourer? Not a bit. It creates capital, i.e., that kind of property which exploits wage labour, and which cannot increase except upon conditions of begetting a new supply of wage labour for fresh exploitation. Property, in its present form, is based on the antagonism of capital and wage labour. Let us examine both sides of this antagonism.

To be a capitalist, is to have not only a purely personal, but a social, *status* in production. Capital is a collective product, and only by the united action of many members, nay, in the last resort, only by the united action of all members of society, can it be set in motion.

Capital is therefore not a personal, it is a social power.

When, therefore, capital is converted into common property, into the property of all members of society, personal property is not thereby transformed into social property. It is only the social character of the property that is changed. It loses its class character.

Let us now take wage labour.

The average price of wage labour is the minimum wage, i.e., that quantum of the means of subsistence which is absolutely requisite to keep the labourer in bare existence as a labourer. What, therefore, the wage labourer appropriates by means of his labour, merely suffices to prolong and reproduce a bare existence. We by no means intend to abolish this personal appropriation of the products of labour, an appropriation that is made for the maintenance and reproduction of human life, and that leaves no surplus wherewith to command the labour of others. All that we want to do away with is the miserable character of this appropriation, under which the labourer lives merely to increase capital, and is allowed to live only in so far as the interest of the ruling class requires it.

In bourgeois society, living labour is but a means to increase accumulated labour. In communist society, accumulated labour is but a means to widen, to enrich, to promote the existence of the labourer.

In bourgeois society, therefore, the past dominates the present; in communist society, the present dominates the past. In bourgeois society capital is independent and has individuality, while the living person is dependent and has no individuality.

And the abolition of this state of things is called by the bourgeois, abolition of individuality and freedom! And rightly so. The abolition of bourgeois individuality, bourgeois independence, and bourgeois freedom is undoubtedly aimed at.

By freedom is meant, under the present bourgeois conditions of production, free trade, free selling and buying.

But if selling and buying disappears, free selling and buying disappears also. This talk about free selling and buying, and all the other "brave words" of our bourgeoisie about freedom in general, have a meaning, if any, only in contrast with restricted selling and buying, with the fettered traders of the Middle Ages, but have no meaning when opposed to the communist abolition of buying and selling, of the bourgeois conditions of production, and of the bourgeoisie itself.

You are horrified at our intending to do away with private property. But in your existing society, private property is already done away with for nine-tenths of the population; its existence for the few is solely due to its non-existence in the hands of those nine-tenths. You reproach us, therefore, with intending to do away with a form of property, the necessary condition for whose existence is the non-existence of any property for the immense majority of society.

In one word, you reproach us with intending to do away with your property. Precisely so; that is just what we intend.

From the moment when labour can no longer be converted into capital, money or rent, into a social power capable of being monopolised, i.e., from the moment when individual property can no longer be transformed into bourgeois property, into capital, from that moment, you say, individuality vanishes.

You must, therefore, confess that by "individual"

you mean no other person than the bourgeois, than the middle-class owner of property. This person must, indeed, be swept out of the way, and made impossible.

Communism deprives no man of the power to appropriate the products of society; all that it does is to deprive him of the power to subjugate the labour of others by means of such appropriation.

It has been objected, that upon the abolition of private property all work will cease, and universal laziness will overtake us.

According to this, bourgeois society ought long ago to have gone to the dogs through sheer idleness; for those of its members who work, acquire nothing, and those who acquire anything, do not work. The whole of this objection is but another expression of the tautology: There can no longer be any wage labour when there is no longer any capital.

All objections urged against the communistic mode of producing and appropriating material products, have, in the same way, been urged against the communistic modes of producing and appropriating intellectual products. Just as to the bourgeois, the disappearance of class property is the disappearance of production itself, so the disappearance of class culture is to him identical with the disappearance of all culture.

That culture, the loss of which he laments, is, for the enormous majority, a mere training to act as a machine.

But don't wrangle with us so long as you apply, to our intended abolition of bourgeois property, the standard of your bourgeois notions of freedom, culture, law, etc.

Your very ideas are but the outgrowth of the conditions of your bourgeois production and bourgeois property, just as your jurisprudence is but the will of your class made into a law for all, a will whose essential character and direction are determined by the economical conditions of existence of your class.

The selfish misconception that induces you to transform into eternal laws of nature and of reason, the social forms springing from your present mode of production and form of property—historical relations that rise and disappear in the progress of production—this misconception you share with every ruling class that has preceded you. What you see clearly in the case of ancient property, what you admit in the case of feudal property, you are of course forbidden to admit in the case of your own bourgeois form of property.

Abolition of the family! Even the most radical flare up at this infamous proposal of the Communists.

On what foundation is the present family, the bourgeois family, based? On capital, on private gain. In its completely developed form this family exists only among the bourgeoisie. But this state of things finds its complement in the practical absence of the family among proletarians, and in public prostitution.

The bourgeois family will vanish as a matter of course when its complement vanishes, and both will vanish with the vanishing of capital.

Do you charge us with wanting to stop the exploitation of children by their parents? To this crime we plead guilty.

But, you will say, we destroy the most hallowed of relations, when we replace home education by social.

And your education! Is not that also social, and determined by the social conditions under which you educate, by the intervention direct or indirect, of society, by means of schools, etc.? The Communists have not invented the intervention of society in education; they do but seek to alter the character of that intervention, and to rescue education from the influence of the ruling class.

The bourgeois claptrap about the family and education, about the hallowed correlation of parent and child, becomes all the more disgusting, the more, by the action of modern industry, all family ties among the proletarians are torn asunder, and their children transformed into simple articles of commerce and instruments of labour.

But you Communists would introduce community of women, screams the whole bourgeoisie in chorus.

The bourgeois sees in his wife a mere instrument of production. He hears that the instruments of production are to be exploited in common, and, naturally, can come to no other conclusion than that the lot of being common to all will likewise fall to the women.

He has not even a suspicion that the real point aimed at is to do away with the status of women as mere instruments of production.

For the rest, nothing is more ridiculous than the virtuous indignation of our bourgeois at the community of women which, they pretend, is to be openly and officially established by the Communists. The Communists have no need to introduce community of women; it has existed almost from time immemorial.

Our bourgeois, not content with having wives and daughters of their proletarians at their disposal, not to speak of common prostitutes, take the greatest pleasure in seducing each other's wives.

Bourgeois marriage is in reality a system of wives in common and thus, at the most, what the Communists might possibly be reproached with is that they desire to introduce, in substitution for a hypocritically concealed, an openly legalised community of women. For the rest, it is self-evident, that the abolition of the present system of production must bring with it the abolition of the community of women springing from that system, i.e., of prostitution both public and private.

The Communists are further reproached with desiring to abolish countries and nationality.

The working men have no country. We cannot take from them what they have not got. Since the proletariat must first of all acquire political supremacy, must rise to be the leading class of the nation, must constitute itself *the* nation, it is, so far, itself national, though not in the bourgeois sense of the word.

National differences and antagonism between peoples are daily more and more vanishing, owing to the development of the bourgeoisie, to freedom of commerce, to the world market, to uniformity in the mode of production and in the conditions of life corresponding thereto.

The supremacy of the proletariat will cause them to vanish still faster. United action of the leading civilised countries at least, is one of the first conditions for the emancipation of the proletariat.

In proportion as the exploitation of one individual by another is put an end to, the exploitation of one nation by another will also be put an end to. In proportion as the antagonism between classes within the nation vanishes, the hostility of one nation to another will come to an end.

The charges against communism made from a religious, a philosophical and, generally, from an ideological standpoint, are not deserving of serious examination.

Does it require deep intuition to comprehend that man's ideas, views, and conceptions, in one word, man's consciousness, changes with every change in the conditions of his material existence, in his social relations and in his social life?

What else does the history of ideas prove, than that intellectual production changes its character in proportion as material production is changed? The ruling ideas of each age have ever been the ideas of its ruling class.

When people speak of ideas that revolutionise society, they do but express the fact that within the old society the elements of a new one have been created, and that the dissolution of the old ideas keeps even pace with the dissolution of the old conditions of existence.

When the ancient world was in its last throes, the ancient religions were overcome by Christianity. When Christian ideas succumbed in the eighteenth century to rationalist ideas, feudal society fought its death battle with the then revolutionary bourgeoisie. The ideas of religious liberty and freedom of conscience, merely gave expression to the sway of free competition within the domain of knowledge.

"Undoubtedly," it will be said, "religious, moral, philosophical and juridical ideas have been modified in the course of historical development. But religion, morality, philosophy, political science, and law, constantly survived this change."

"There are, besides, eternal truths, such as Freedom, Justice, etc., that are common to all states of society. But communism abolishes eternal truths, it abolishes all religion, and all morality, instead of constituting them on a new basis; it therefore acts in contradiction to all past historical experience."

What does this accusation reduce itself to? The history of all past society has consisted in the development of class antagonisms, antagonisms that assumed different forms at different epochs.

But whatever form they may have taken, one fact is common to all past ages, viz., the exploitation of one part of society by the other. No wonder, then, that the social consciousness of past ages, despite all the multiplicity and variety it displays, moves within certain common forms, or general ideas, which cannot completely vanish except with the total disappearance of class antagonisms.

The communist revolution is the most radical rupture with traditional relations; no wonder that its development involves the most radical rupture with traditional ideas.

But let us have done with the bourgeois objections to communism.

We have seen above that the first step in the revolution by the working class is to raise the proletariat to the position of ruling class to win the battle of democracy.

The proletariat will use its political supremacy to wrest, by degrees, all capital from the bourgeoisie, to centralise all instruments of production in the hands of the state, i.e., of the proletariat organised as the ruling class; and to increase the total of productive forces as rapidly as possible.

Of course, in the beginning, this cannot be effected except by means of despotic inroads on the rights of property, and on the conditions of bourgeois production; by means of measures, therefore, which appear economically insufficient and untenable, but which, in the course of the movement, outstrip themselves, necessitate further inroads upon the old social order, and are unavoidable as a means of entirely revolutionising the mode of production.

These measures will of course be different in different countries.

Nevertheless, in the most advanced countries, the following will be pretty generally applicable.

1. Abolition of property in land and application of all rents of land to public purposes.

2. A heavy progressive or graduated income tax.

3. Abolition of all right of inheritance.

4. Confiscation of the property of all emigrants and rebels.

5. Centralisation of credit in the hands of the state, by means of a national bank with state capital and an exclusive monopoly.

6. Centralisation of the means of communication and transport in the hands of the state.

7. Extension of factories and instruments of production owned by the state; the bringing into cultivation of waste lands, and the improvement of the soil generally in accordance with a common plan.

8. Equal obligation of all to work. Establishment of industrial armies, especially for agriculture.

9. Combination of agriculture with manufacturing industries; gradual abolition of all the distinction between town and country by a more equable distribution of the population over the country.

10. Free education for all children in public schools. Abolition of children's factory labour in its present form. Combination of education with industrial production, etc.

When, in the course of development, class distinctions have disappeared, and all production has been concentrated in the hands of a vast association of the whole nation, the public power will lose its political character. Political power, properly so called, is merely the organised power of one class for oppressing another. If the proletariat during its contest with the bourgeoisie is compelled, by the force of circumstances, to organise itself as a class; if, by means of a revolution, it makes itself the ruling class, and, as such, sweeps away by force the old conditions of production, then it will, along with these conditions, have swept away the conditions for the existence of class antagonisms and of classes generally, and will thereby have abolished its own supremacy as a class.

In place of the old bourgeois society, with its classes and class antagonisms, we shall have an association in which the free development of each is the condition for the free development of all.

III. SOCIALIST AND COMMUNIST LITERATURE

1. REACTIONARY SOCIALISM

a. Feudal Socialism

Owing to their historical position it became the vocation of the aristocracies of France and England to write pamphlets against modern bourgeois society. In the French Revolution of July, 1830, and in the English reform agitation, these aristocracies again succumbed to the hateful upstart. Thenceforth a serious political struggle was altogether out of the question. A literary battle alone remained possible. But even in the domain of literature the old cries of the restoration period* had become impossible.

In order to arouse sympathy the aristocracy was obliged to lose sight, apparently, of its own interests, and to formulate its indictment against the bourgeoisie in the interest of the exploited working class alone. Thus the aristocracy took their revenge by singing lampoons on their new master and whispering in his ears sinister prophecies of coming catastrophe.

In this way arose feudal socialism: half lamentation, half lampoon; half echo of the past, half menace of the future; at times, by its bitter, witty and incisive criticism, striking the bourgeoisie to the very heart's core, but always ludicrous in its effect, through total incapacity to comprehend the march of modern history.

The aristocracy, in order to rally the people to them, waved the proletarian alms-bag in front for a banner. But the people, so often as it joined them, saw on their hindquarters the old feudal coats of arms, and deserted with loud and irreverent laughter.

One section of the French Legitimists and "Young England" exhibited this spectacle.

In pointing out that their mode of exploitation was different to that of the bourgeoisie, the feudalists forget that they exploited under circumstances and conditions that were quite different and that are now antiquated. In showing that, under their rule, the modern proletariat

---

*Not the English Restoration, 1660 to 1689, but the French Restoration, 1814 to 1830. [*Note by F. Engels to the English edition of* 1888.]

never existed, they forget that the modern bourgeoisie is the necessary offspring of their own form of society.

For the rest, so little do they conceal the reactionary character of their criticism that their chief accusation against the bourgeoisie amounts to this, that under the bourgeois régime a class is being developed which is destined to cut up root and branch the old order of society.

What they upbraid the bourgeoisie with is not so much that it creates a proletariat as that it creates a *revolutionary* proletariat.

In political practice, therefore, they join in all coercive measures against the working class; and in ordinary life, despite their high falutin' phrases, they stoop to pick up the golden apples dropped from the tree of industry, and to barter truth, love, and honour for traffic in wool, beetroot-sugar, and potato spirits.*

As the parson has ever gone hand in hand with the landlord, so has clerical socialism with feudal socialism.

Nothing is easier than to give Christian asceticism a socialist tinge. Has not Christianity declaimed against private property, against marriage, against the state? Has it not preached in the place of these, charity and

---

*This applies chiefly to Germany where the landed aristocracy and squirearchy have large portions of their estates cultivated for their own account by stewards, and are, moreover, extensive beetroot-sugar manufacturers and distillers of potato spirits. The wealthier British aristocracy are, as yet, rather above that; but they, too, know how to make up for declining rents by lending their names to floaters of more or less shady joint-stock companies. [*Note by F. Engels to the English edition of* 1888.]

poverty, celibacy and mortification of the flesh, monastic life and Mother Church? Christian socialism is but the holy water with which the priest consecrates the heart-burnings of the aristocrat.

b. Petty-Bourgeois Socialism

The feudal aristocracy was not the only class that was ruined by the bourgeoisie, not the only class whose conditions of existence pined and perished in the atmosphere of modern bourgeois society. The medieval burgesses and the small peasant proprietors were the precursors of the modern bourgeoisie. In those countries which are but little developed, industrially and commercially, these two classes still vegetate side by side with the rising bourgeoisie.

In countries where modern civilisation has become fully developed, a new class of petty bourgeois has been formed, fluctuating between proletariat and bourgeoisie, and ever renewing itself as a supplementary part of bourgeois society. The individual members of this class, however, are being constantly hurled down into the proletariat by the action of competition, and, as modern industry develops, they even see the moment approaching when they will completely disappear as an independent section of modern society, to be replaced, in manufactures, agriculture and commerce, by overlookers, bailiffs and shopmen.

In countries like France, where the peasants constitute far more than half of the population, it was natural that writers who sided with the proletariat against the bourgeoisie should use, in their criticism of the bourgeois régime, the standard of the peasant and petty bourgeois, and from the standpoint of these intermediate classes should take up the cudgels for the working class. Thus arose petty-bourgeois socialism. Sismondi was the head of this school, not only in France but also in England.

This school of socialism dissected with great acuteness the contradictions in the conditions of modern production. It laid bare the hypocritical apologies of economists. It proved, incontrovertibly, the disastrous effects of machinery and division of labour; the concentration of capital and land in a few hands; over-production and crises; it pointed out the inevitable ruin of the petty bourgeois and peasant, the misery of the proletariat, the anarchy in production, the crying inequalities in the distribution of wealth, the industrial war of extermination between nations, the dissolution of old moral bonds, of the old family relations, of the old nationalities.

In its positive aims, however, this form of socialism aspires either to restoring the old means of production and of exchange, and with them the old property relations, and the old society, or to cramping the modern means of production and of exchange within the framework of the old property relations that have been, and were bound to be, exploded by those means. In either case it is both reactionary and utopian.

Its last words are: Corporate guilds for manufacture; patriarchal relations in agriculture.

Ultimately, when stubborn historical facts had dispersed all intoxicating effect of self-deception, this form of socialism ended in a miserable fit of the blues.

c. German or "True" Socialism

The socialist and communist literature of France, a literature that originated under the pressure of a bourgeoisie in power, and that was the expression of the struggle against this power, was introduced into Germany at a time when the bourgeoisie in that country had just begun its contest with feudal absolutism.

German philosophers, would-be philosophers and men of letters eagerly seized on this literature, only forgetting that when these writings immigrated from France into Germany, French social conditions had not immigrated along with them. In contact with German social conditions this French literature lost all its immediate practical significance and assumed a purely literary aspect. Thus, to the German philosophers of the eighteenth century, the demands of the first French Revolution were nothing more than the demands of "Practical Reason" in general, and the utterance of the will of the revolutionary French bourgeoisie signified in their eyes the laws of pure will, of will as it was bound to be, of true human will generally.

The work of the German *literati* consisted solely in bringing the new French ideas into harmony with their ancient philosophical conscience, or rather, in annexing the French ideas without deserting their own philosophic point of view.

This annexation took place in the same way in which a foreign language is appropriated, namely, by translation.

It is well known how the monks wrote silly lives of Catholic saints *over* the manuscripts on which the classical works of ancient heathendom had been written. The German *literati* reversed this process with the profane French literature. They wrote their philosophical nonsense beneath the French original. For instance, beneath the French criticism of the economic functions of money, they wrote "alienation of humanity," and beneath the French criticism of the bourgeois state they wrote "dethronement of the category of the general," and so forth.

The introduction of these philosophical phrases at the back of the French historical criticisms they dubbed "Philosophy of Action," "True Socialism," "German Science of Socialism," "Philosophical Foundation of Socialism," and so on.

The French socialist and communist literature was thus completely emasculated. And, since it ceased in the hands of the German to express the struggle of one class with the other, he felt conscious of having overcome "French one-sidedness" and of representing, not true requirements, but the requirements of truth; not the interests of the proletariat, but the interests of human nature, of man in general, who belongs to no class, has no reality, who exists only in the misty realm of philosophical phantasy.

This German socialism, which took its schoolboy task so seriously and solemnly, and extolled its poor stock-in-trade in such mountebank fashion, meanwhile gradually lost its pedantic innocence.

The fight of the German and especially of the Prussian bourgeoisie against feudal aristocracy and absolute monarchy, in other words, the liberal movement, became more earnest.

By this, the long-wished-for opportunity was offered to "True" Socialism of confronting the political movement with the socialist demands, of hurling the traditional anathemas against liberalism, against representative government, against bourgeois competition, bourgeois freedom of the press, bourgeois legislation, bourgeois liberty and equality, and of preaching to the masses that they had nothing to gain, and everything to lose, by this bourgeois movement. German socialism forgot, in the nick of time, that the French criticism, whose silly echo it was, presupposed the existence of modern bourgeois society, with its corresponding economic conditions of existence, and the political constitution adapted thereto, the very things whose attainment was the object of the pending struggle in Germany.

To the absolute governments, with their following of parsons, professors, country squires and officials, it served as a welcome scarecrow against the threatening bourgeoisie.

It was a sweet finish after the bitter pills of floggings and bullets, with which these same governments, just at that time, dosed the German working-class risings.

While this "True" Socialism thus served the governments as a weapon for fighting the German bourgeoisie, it, at the same time, directly represented a reactionary interest, the interest of the German philistines. In Germany the petty-bourgeois class, a relic of the sixteenth century, and since then constantly cropping up again under the various forms, is the real social basis of the existing state of things.

To preserve this class is to preserve the existing state of things in Germany. The industrial and political supremacy of the bourgeoisie threatens it with certain destruction—on the one hand, from the concentration of capital; on the other, from the rise of a revolutionary proletariat. "True" Socialism appeared to kill these two birds with one stone. It spread like an epidemic.

The robe of speculative cobwebs, embroidered with flowers of rhetoric, steeped in the dew of sickly sentiment, this transcendental robe in which the German Socialists wrapped their sorry "eternal truths," all skin and bone, served to wonderfully increase the sale of their goods amongst such a public. And on its part German socialism recognised, more and more, its own calling as the bombastic representative of the petty-bourgeois philistine.

It proclaimed the German nation to be the model nation, and the German petty philistine to be the typical man. To every villainous meanness of this model man it gave a hidden, higher, socialistic interpretation, the exact contrary of its real character. It went to the extreme length of directly opposing the "brutally destructive" tendency of communism, and of proclaiming its supreme and impartial contempt of all class struggles.

With very few exceptions all the so-called socialist and communist publications that now (1847) circulate in Germany belong to the domain of this foul and enervating literature.*

2. CONSERVATIVE OR BOURGEOIS SOCIALISM

A part of the bourgeoisie is desirous of redressing social grievances in order to secure the continued existence of bourgeois society.

To this section belong economists, philanthropists, humanitarians, improvers of the condition of the working class, organisers of charity, members of societies for the prevention of cruelty to animals, temperance fanatics, hole-and-corner reformers of every imaginable kind. This form of socialism has, moreover, been worked out into complete systems.

We may cite Proudhon's *Philosophie de la Misère* [*Philosophy of Poverty*] as an example of this form.

The socialistic bourgeois want all the advantages of modern social conditions without the struggles and dangers necessarily resulting therefrom. They desire the existing state of society minus its revolutionary and disintegrating elements. They wish for a bourgeoisie

---

*The revolutionary storm of 1848 swept away this whole shabby tendency and cured its protagonists of the desire to dabble in socialism. The chief representative and classical type of this tendency is Mr. Karl Grün. [*Note by F. Engels to the German edition of* 1888.]

without a proletariat. The bourgeoisie naturally conceives the world in which it is supreme to be the best; and bourgeois socialism develops this comfortable conception into various more or less complete systems. In requiring the proletariat to carry out such a system, and thereby to march straightway into the social New Jerusalem, it but requires in reality that the proletariat should remain within the bounds of existing society, but should cast away all its hateful ideas concerning the bourgeoisie.

A second and more practical, but less systematic, form of this socialism sought to depreciate every revolutionary movement in the eyes of the working class by showing that no mere political reform, but only a change in the material conditions of existence, in economical relations, could be of any advantage to them. By changes in the material conditions of existence, this form of socialism, however, by no means understands abolition of the bourgeois relations of production, an abolition that can be effected only by a revolution, but administrative reforms, based on the continued existence of these relations; reforms, therefore, that in no respect affect the relations between capital and labour, but, at the best, lessen the cost, and simplify the administrative work of bourgeois government.

Bourgeois socialism attains adequate expression when, and only when, it becomes a mere figure of speech.

Free trade: for the benefit of the working class. Protective duties: for the benefit of the working class. Prison reform: for the benefit of the working class. This is the last word and the only seriously meant word of bourgeois socialism.

It is summed up in the phrase: the bourgeois is a bourgeois—for the benefit of the working class.

3. CRITICAL-UTOPIAN SOCIALISM AND COMMUNISM

We do not here refer to that literature which, in every great modern revolution, has always given voice to the demands of the proletariat, such as the writings of Babeuf and others.

The first direct attempts of the proletariat to attain its own ends, made in times of universal excitement, when feudal society was being overthrown; these attempts necessarily failed, owing to the then undeveloped state of the proletariat, as well as to the absence of the economic conditions for its emancipation, conditions that had yet to be produced, and could be produced by the impending bourgeois epoch alone. The revolutionary literature that accompanied these first movements of the proletariat had necessarily a reactionary character. It inculcated universal asceticism and social levelling in its crudest form.

The socialist and communist systems, properly so called, those of Saint-Simon, Fourier, Owen, and others, spring into existence in the early undeveloped period, described above, of the struggle between proletariat and bourgeoisie (see Section 1. Bourgeois and Proletarians).

The founders of these systems see, indeed, the class antagonisms, as well as the action of the decomposing elements in the prevailing form of society. But the proletariat, as yet in its infancy, offers to them the spectacle of a class without any historical initiative or any independent political movement.

Since the development of class antagonism keeps even pace with the development of industry, the economic situation, as they find it, does not as yet offer to them the material conditions for the emancipation of the proletariat. They therefore search after a new social science, after new social laws, that are to create these conditions.

Historical action is to yield to their personal inventive action; historically created conditions of emancipation to fantastic ones; and the gradual, spontaneous class organisation of the proletariat to an organisation of society especially contrived by these inventors. Future history resolves itself, in their eyes, into the propaganda and the practical carrying out of their social plans.

In the formation of their plans they are conscious of caring chiefly for the interests of the working class, as being the most suffering class. Only from the point of view of being the most suffering class does the proletariat exist for them.

The undeveloped state of the class struggle, as well as their own surroundings, causes Socialists of this kind to consider themselves far superior to all class antagonisms. They want to improve the condition of every member of society, even that of the most favoured. Hence, they habitually appeal to society at large, without distinction of class; nay, by preference, to the ruling class. For how can people, when once they understand their system, fail to see in it the best possible plan of the best possible state of society?

Hence, they reject all political, and especially all revolutionary action; they wish to attain their ends by peaceful means, and endeavour, by small experiments, necessarily doomed to failure, and by the force of example, to pave the way for the new social gospel.

Such fantastic pictures of future society, painted at a time when the proletariat is still in a very undeveloped state and has but a fantastic conception of its own position, correspond with the first instinctive yearnings of that class for a general reconstruction of society.

But these socialist and communist publications contain also a critical element. They attack every principle of existing society. Hence they are full of the most valuable materials for the enlightenment of the working class. The practical measures proposed in them—such as the abolition of the distinction between town and country, of the family, of the carrying on of industries for the account of private individuals, and of the wage system, the proclamation of social harmony, the conversion of the function of the state into a mere superintendence of production—all these proposals point solely to the disappearance of class antagonisms which were, at that time, only just cropping up, and which, in these publications, are recognised in their earliest indistinct and undefined forms only. These proposals, therefore, are of a purely utopian character.

The significance of critical-utopian socialism and communism bears an inverse relation to historical development. In proportion as the modern class struggle develops and takes definite shape, this fantastic standing apart from the contest, these fantastic attacks on it, lose all practical value and all theoretical justification. Therefore, although the originators of these systems were, in many respects, revolutionary, their disciples have, in every case, formed mere reactionary sects. They hold fast by the original views of their masters, in opposition to the progressive historical development of the proletariat. They, therefore, endeavour, and that consistently, to deaden the class struggle and to reconcile the class antagonisms. They still dream of experimental realisation of their social utopias, of founding isolated *phalanstères*, of establishing "Home Colonies," or setting up a "Little Icaria"*—pocket editions of the New Jerusalem—and to realise all these castles in the air they are compelled to appeal to the feelings and purses of the bourgeois. By degrees they sink into the category of the reactionary conservative socialists depicted above, differing from these only by more systematic pedantry, and by their fanatical and superstitious belief in the miraculous effects of their social science.

They, therefore, violently oppose all political action

*"Home colonies" were what Owen called his communist model societies. [*Added by F. Engels to the German edition of* 1890.] *Phalanstères* were socialist colonies on the plan of Charles Fourier; Icaria was the name given by Caber to his utopia and, later on, to his American communist colony. [*Note by F. Engels to the English edition of* 1888.]

on the part of the working class; such action, according to them, can only result from blind unbelief in the new gospel.

The Owenites in England, and the Fourierists in France, respectively, oppose the Chartists and the *Réformistes*.

IV. POSITION OF THE COMMUNISTS IN RELATION TO THE VARIOUS EXISTING OPPOSITION PARTIES

Section II has made clear the relations of the Communists to the existing working-class parties, such as the Chartists in England and the Agrarian Reformers in America.

The Communists fight for the attainment of the immediate aims, for the enforcement of the momentary interests of the working class; but in the movement of the present they also represent and take care of the future of that movement. In France the Communists ally themselves with the Social-Democrats* against the conser-

---

*The party then represented in Parliament by Ledru-Rollin, in literature by Louis Blanc (1811–82), in the daily press by the *Réforme*. The name of Social-Democracy signifies, with these its inventors, a section of the Democratic or Republican Party more or less tinged with socialism. [*Note by F. Engels to the English edition of 1888.*]

vative and radical bourgeoisie, reserving, however, the right to take up a critical position in regard to phrases and illusions traditionally handed down from the Great Revolution.

In Switzerland they support the Radicals, without losing sight of the fact that this party consists of antagonistic elements, partly of Democratic Socialists, in the French sense, partly of radical bourgeois.

In Poland they support the party that insists on an agrarian revolution as the prime condition for national emancipation, that party which fomented the insurrection of Cracow in 1846.

In Germany they fight with the bourgeoisie whenever it acts in a revolutionary way, against the absolute monarchy, the feudal squirearchy, and the petty-bourgeoisie.

But they never cease, for a single instant, to instil into the working class the clearest possible recognition of the hostile antagonism between bourgeoisie and proletariat, in order that the German workers may straightway use, as so many weapons against the bourgeoisie, the social and political conditions that the bourgeoisie must necessarily introduce along with its supremacy, and in order that, after the fall of the reactionary classes in Germany, the fight against the bourgeoisie itself may immediately begin.

The Communists turn their attention chiefly to Germany, because that country is on the eve of a bourgeois revolution that is bound to be carried out under more advanced conditions of European civilisation and with a much more developed proletariat than that of England was in the seventeenth, and of France in the eighteenth century, and because the bourgeois revolution in Germany will be but the prelude to an immediately following proletarian revolution.

In short, the Communists everywhere support every revolutionary movement against the existing social and political order of things.

In all these movements they bring to the front, as the leading question in each, the property question, no matter what its degree of development at the time.

Finally, they labour everywhere for the union and agreement of the democratic parties of all countries.

The Communists disdain to conceal their views and aims. They openly declare that their ends can be attained only by the forcible overthrow of all existing social conditions. Let the ruling classes tremble at a communist revolution. The proletarians have nothing to lose but their chains. They have a world to win.

Working men of all countries, unite!

AFTERWORD
KARL MARX'S CRYSTAL BALL

In February 1848, Karl Marx was a twenty-nine-year-old university-educated journalist; his collaborator, Friedrich Engels, was twenty-seven. Their *Communist Manifesto*, published that month, was composed in Brussels—the capital of today's European Union—and printed in London. Marx, consulting some prior writings of Engels, wrote the text.* He barely made his deadline (and may have pulled some all-nighters); in fact, he did not even finish the last section. Largely ignored in its day, the book has had an astonishing afterlife.

Most readers would associate *The Communist Manifesto* with its denunciation of private property and wage labor, as well as its political prescriptions for radical revolution—which proved catastrophic for humanity. Murderous Communist regimes in the twentieth century must factor into any assessment of Marx's ideas and their role in

*Terrel Carver, *Marx and Engels: The Intellectual Relationship* (Bloomington: Indiana University, 1983), chap. 3.

history.* Still, *The Communist Manifesto* brims with lyricism about the magic of modern capitalism, and remains perhaps the greatest tribute ever to capitalism's power.

Admittedly, such a distinction is usually bestowed upon Adam Smith's *Wealth of Nations* (1776), which offered enduring arguments on behalf of competition, specialization (the division of labor), and the power of self-interest to increase social betterment. Marx read Smith's influential treatise on markets and morals, as did many contemporaries of Smith, such as James Madison, Alexander Hamilton, and Thomas Jefferson. Smith's overall perspective has triumphed historically. And yet his lengthy masterpiece is filled with sometimes difficult, archaic eighteenth-century prose. Marx's short, snappy text is more accessible, and his vision of capitalism more global.

Let us listen:

Steam and machinery revolutionised industrial production. The place of manufacture was taken by the giant, modern industry, the place of the industrial middle class by industrial millionaires.... Modern industry has established the world market, for which the discovery of America paved the way. This market has given an immense development to commerce, to navigation, to communication by land ... as indus-

*Leszek Kołakowski, "Marxist Roots of Stalinism," in Robert C. Tucker (ed.), *Stalinism: Essays in Historical Interpretation* (New York: Norton, 1977), 283–98; Kołakowski "New York Times: Editorial of May 8, 1975: 30th Anniversary of the New Order in Europe: Victory for Common Sense!" *Survey*, 21/4 (1975): 87–9.

try, commerce, navigation, railways extended, in the same proportion the bourgeoisie developed, [and] increased its capital.   (pages 64–65)

What is most remarkable about this and other such vivid passages is that their descriptions were mostly *of the future.* When Marx was writing, "giant, modern industry" and the "world market" were in their infancy. But he grasped the structural drivers pushing toward the first great globalization. Marx also captured the disruption inherent in modern capitalism's ability to destroy and to create. In both those senses—globalization and capitalism's relentless upheaval—*The Communist Manifesto* speaks directly to our time.

THE FIRST GREAT GLOBALIZATION
(1870s–1920s)

"The need of a constantly expanding market for
its products chases the bourgeoisie over the whole
surface of the globe. It must nestle everywhere, settle
everywhere, establish connections everywhere."

—*The Communist Manifesto* (page 67)

The verb "globalize" is first attested by the *Merriam-Webster Dictionary* in 1944, but even into the 1970s writers who employed the term considered it novel.* As for the noun "globalization," it has only been commonplace since the 1990s. Still, the phenomenon of globalization is older than the terminology.

Some analysts date the onset of the first great globalization from the invention of steam: by the 1830s, steam-powered ships (soon made of iron) operated on rivers and oceans, using coaling stations that would be deployed around the world. In 1869, the Suez Canal—connecting the Mediterranean and the Red seas, and thereby vastly shortening travel from Europe to Asia—was opened primarily for steamships.†

Other analysts point to the first transatlantic (underwater) telegraph cable laid in 1866, followed by similar cables in the 1870s from Britain to India, China, Japan, and Australia, East and South Africa. By 1880, big shots in London could communicate, in real time, with the United States or any part of the British Empire. This also had huge implications for the relaying of news, and the onset of war. In 1914, Austria-Hungary declared war against Serbia by telegraph, setting off the First World War.

Still others look to the development of overseas markets. In 1851, Isaac Merritt Singer established his sewing machine company and four years later set up an affiliate in Paris, launching one of the first U.S. multina-

*George Modelski, *Principles of World Politics* (New York: Free Press, 1972).
†Stephen Kern, *The Culture of Time and Space, 1880–1918* (Cambridge, MA: Harvard University, 1983).

tional corporations. Within six years, foreign revenues of Singer Sewing Co. exceeded U.S. revenues. Other American companies would soon beat the global path, too, like John Rockefeller's Standard Oil. By 1913, *World-Economy Archive* was founded, in Kiel, Germany, as the first journal with a focus on genuinely global economics.

Whatever marker we select for the beginnings of the first great globalization, it is clear that by the 1870s—when *The Communist Manifesto* happened to be republished— new technologies were dramatically lowering transportation and communication costs.* Marx had caught the long-term direction and scope of this transformation.

Marx was also prescient about the onset of "giant, modern industry." Huge changes followed not only the advent of steam power but also the invention in the 1850s of processes to manufacture steel, a strong and elastic form of iron. New industrial chemicals, too, were invented and mass manufactured in the decades after *The Communist Manifesto*: chlorine bleach for making cotton, synthetic dyes for coloring clothes, synthetic fertilizers for increasing crop yields. In 1866, the father of the Nobel Peace Prize, Alfred Nobel, invented nitroglycerine (dynamite), an explosive that transformed railroad construction and mining. World steel production— which was predicated upon mining iron ore and coking coal—skyrocketed from 71,000 tons in 1850 to 500,000 tons in 1870 and 28 million tons by 1900. Steel would

---

*Eric J. Hobsbawm, *The Age of Capital, 1848–1875* (New York: Charles Scribner's, 1975).

revolutionize war, with artillery and tanks, as well as civilian life, with skyscrapers and subways.

As for Marx's "world market," world trade had doubled between 1800 and 1850, but between 1850 and 1913 it expanded *tenfold*.

Marx's comments on the revolution of the railroads deserve special mention as well. The world of Marx and Engels had no coordinated time. Time differences between locales were set without rhyme or reason, according to the whims of local officials. In the 1880s, Helmuth von Moltke, the great German general, called for the introduction of a global standard time, arguing that it was necessary to have reliable time to coordinate troop movements and operational plans for wars. Moltke's desires were enacted by railroad companies.

Prospective passengers (customers) had to know when the trains would arrive and depart any given station, but New York was a crazy eleven minutes and forty-five seconds behind Boston. At noon in Chicago, it was eleven fifty a.m. in St. Louis and twelve eighteen p.m. in Detroit. In 1883, however, railroads in the United States divided North America into four time zones with standardized clocks throughout each zone—what became known as "railroad time." The next year, an international conference in Washington, D.C., called for Greenwich, England, to be made "zero time," and for the rest of the world to be divided into twenty-four units, each one hour apart. At first, twenty-five countries agreed to the world time zones. By 1913, the system had been adopted almost everywhere.

Marx was not the only observer to recognize incipient globalization, but he was among the earliest. Sixty-three years after *The Communist Manifesto*, Norman Angell, a British-born writer, published his own manifesto about how world integration could not be stopped. Appearing in twenty-five languages and selling more than 2 million copies worldwide, the book was entitled *The Great Illusion*, which referred to the diminishment of military power compared with newfound economic power. A few years later, the First World War broke out. Millions of people died, as would the first great globalization.* Still, Angell's work testified to the profound impression made by the deep global integration that Marx's manifesto saw coming.

The stepped-up global interconnectedness after 1870 led to a stark division between a few advantaged industrializers (western Europe, North America, Japan) and legions of raw material suppliers (sub-Saharan Africa, South America, much of Asia)—an unequal form of specialization, different from the kind described by Adam Smith. True, the world's division into a richer North and a poorer South, paradoxically, enhanced the sense of there being one interconnected world. But such inequality was then, and is again today, one of the bases for critiques of globalization, or at least of certain types of globalization—an ongoing multisided debate.†

---

*Harold James, *The End of Globalization: Lessons from the Great Depression* (Cambridge, MA: Harvard University, 2001).

†David Held et al., *Debating Globalization* (Cambridge, UK: Polity, 2005).

THE RELENTLESS UPHEAVAL
OF CAPITALISM

"The bourgeoisie cannot exist without constantly
revolutionising the instruments of production ... and
with them the whole relations of society."

          —*The Communist Manifesto* (page 67)

The "bourgeois" Angell was born in England, attended
lycée in France, did further studies in Switzerland, and at
age seventeen emigrated to California, where he planted
vines, prospected for gold, and became a journalist, before
resettling in Paris and then moving back to England. His
life was extraordinary—he would win one of Nobel's
Peace Prizes—yet fully in keeping with the radical
possibilities Marx described. The period not long after
The Communist Manifesto was an epoch of profound
global mobility of goods, but also of people.

Nowadays, amid the second great globalization
(1950s–present), which many people mistakenly regard as unprecedented, most of the world's people have
never lived or worked in another country. As of 2000,
only about 3 percent of the global population lived outside their country of birth or citizenship (a little over
200 million out of more than 6.5 billion). Many millions
of those outside their countries of origin were tempo-

rary refugees, driven out by war or natural disaster, and hoping to return.

In the decades following *The Communist Manifesto*, however, the world experienced radical mass migration without return. Between 1870 and 1925, probably up to one-seventh of the world's working-age population moved permanently to another country. The first great globalization not only created a world economy, but fundamentally altered people's sense of opportunity.

Migrants from Europe traveled mostly to the United States (some 32 million), but many went to Brazil, Argentina, and Cuba, as well as to Africa, Australia, and New Zealand. Four million Italians crossed to Argentina in the 1880s and 1890s; some worked and went home, but most stayed. About 1.4 million Swedish first- and second-generation immigrants were listed as living in the U.S. as of 1910, when Sweden's population was 5.5 million. So roughly one-fifth of all Swedes alive in the world had their permanent homes in America.

This great European migration to the Americas is well-known. Less known may be the fact that between the 1840s and 1940s, 50 million people flowed into the Malay Peninsula and Burma (both British colonies), the Dutch Indies (Indonesia), and the South Pacific. These migrants came from India (29 million) and China (19 million), with a few million coming from Africa and the Middle East.*

*Adam McKeown, "Global Migration, 1846–1940," *Journal of World History*, 15/2 (2004): 155–90.

Asians resettled permanently in the Americas, too. Japanese laborers migrated to Peru to mine guano for fertilizer and to Hawaii to harvest sugar, while Chinese and Koreans also went to Hawaii (and to Siberia). A few million Asians uprooted themselves on indentured-labor contracts ("coolies") to California, as well as to South Africa, Cuba, British Columbia, the Guyanas, the Dutch Indies, and elsewhere, to work on plantations or in construction.

Movement within the largest countries was no less spectacular: about 30 million Chinese moved to Chinese-controlled Manchuria in the late nineteenth and early twentieth centuries; about 10 million Russian subjects moved inside the Russian empire to Siberia and Turkestan (Central Asia). Whether migrants ventured on the high seas or roughed it across land, the vast majority were looking for opportunity. They took big risks.

Increased risk and disruption constituted one of the great themes of *The Communist Manifesto*, and here, too, Marx was on target. The advent of electricity initially meant soaring demand for copper (wires), drawing Montana, Chile, and Southern Africa into the world economy, offering a possible path to prosperity. But if copper became oversupplied in any given year, or demand suddenly slackened, those places would be thrown into turmoil. The same was true for Bolivia (tin), Ivory Coast (cocoa), Cuba (sugar), Indonesia (rubber): all these places became linked to global markets, and therefore subject to wild commodity price swings—radically affecting livelihoods, up and down.

The consequences of global integration were enormous: the collapse of one bank in the Austro-Hungarian Empire in 1873 triggered a depression that spread as far as the United States, causing mass unemployment. A phenomenal wealth machine, capitalism under conditions of global interdependence was also destabilizing, often for better, but also for worse, giving rise to what Marx labeled a new "everlasting uncertainty" (page 67).

Uncertainty escalated for peasants as much as, if not more than, for bankers. Three waves of drought, famine, and disease (1876–79, 1889–91, 1896–1900) claimed the lives of 30 to 60 million people in India, China, and Brazil. The 15 million people who died of famine in British India were equivalent to half the population of England at the time. Florence Nightingale, the famous nurse, wrote in 1877 of "a hideous record of human suffering and destruction the world has never seen before." Had such mass death—the equivalent of thirty Irish famines or sixty Battles of the Somme (WWI)—occurred in Europe, it would be regarded as a central episode of world history.*

What happened? Something Marx did not grasp, but that we, in our climate-sensitive age, can easily appreciate. The airflows of El Niño—the recurrent warming of the Pacific Ocean—export heat and humidity to other parts of the world, creating an unstable climate for farming. The resulting torrential rains, floods, landslides, severe

---

*Mike Davis, *Late Victorian Holocausts: El Niño, Famines, and the Making of the Third World* (London and New York: Verso, 2001).

droughts, and wildfires often devastated peasant crops. Still, the Victorian-era starvation need not have been so bad. In fact, many places had food surpluses, but these regions had recently experienced commercialization—that is, a deeper involvement in the world-market economy, including specialization away from subsistence agriculture. Progress (the spread of the market) had made possible generous increases in production in good times, but progress also undermined traditional methods for coping with cyclical drought. In addition, colonial rulers compounded the new market uncertainties with inept and racist rule, preventing adequate famine relief.

Marx would have blamed capitalism itself. In this he would have been wrong: the tyranny of imperialism was separate from capitalism. (Capitalism has thrived following global decolonization.) Nonetheless, Marx understood that capitalism was radical in its power to destroy and to create. "All old-established national industries have been destroyed or are daily being destroyed," he wrote. "They are dislodged by new industries, whose introduction becomes a life and death question for all civilised nations" (page 68). In other words, not only did industries compete in a struggle to survive, but countries needed to have the most competitive industries—or risk being conquered.

Capitalism's volatility and disruption could be brutal, but Marx recognized that competitive destruction allowed for great innovation and material advance. Ultimately, he, along with many others, dreamed of removing capitalism's devastating displacements and risk, while retaining its fantastic creative force. Today, various possible steps for melioration are put forth by people of liberal persuasion. For people of conservative persuasion, curbing capitalism's built-in excesses is generally viewed as near impossible, and even to try is seen as causing more harm than good.

HISTORY'S MIDDLE CLASSES

In the end, what are we to make of *The Communist Manifesto*? We should never forget that it was a political tract, spirited but full of wishful thinking (imminent revolution), influential but based on a dangerously flawed theory of history.

That a self-styled "scientific socialist" such as Marx championed capitalism's productive power was no accident. He followed the German philosopher Georg Wilhelm Friedrich Hegel in believing that history moved in stages through contradictions toward an end goal (telos). Specifically, Marx thought history entailed a progression from feudalism to capitalism, then capitalism to socialism, and finally the telos of history—communism. That is why he called himself a Communist while advocating for socialism: a Communist first had to build socialism. But before that, capitalism had to make socialism possible by achieving high-level economic development.

The transition to socialism (and on to communism), therefore, was supposed to occur in the most advanced, already prosperous countries. Marx never fully explained what would then happen to the less advanced countries—would they have to go through a full stage of capitalism before being able to make the transition to socialism? Or, would they be able to leap straight from primitive capitalism, or even semifeudalism, directly to socialism? The latter answer was adopted by Lenin and his successor, Stalin, and by Mao. Their Soviet Communist and Chinese Communist regimes, respectively, killed tens of millions in civil wars, famines, and state-led social engineering.

No advanced country has ever made "a transition" to the kind of socialism called for by Marx—the socialism without private property, wage labor, or a market economy. Instead, in the kind of competition celebrated in *The Communist Manifesto*, the capitalist market economies of countries like the United States crushed the socialist economies of the Communist Soviet Union and its satellite states in Eastern Europe. With the 1991 Soviet collapse, the specter of *The Communist Manifesto* ceased to haunt humanity.

Capitalism seems as powerful as ever. The key to that power has not been some narrow "bourgeoisie" (or "capital"), as Marx imagined, but broad middle classes. And the latter did not act as some unified class pursuing its class interests—such a collective actor is a fiction—but rather, as Adam Smith suggested, people of the middle classes mostly pursued individual self-interest.

Marx erred even more grievously in forecasting the disappearance of the middle classes. Following *The Communist Manifesto*, middle-class life would enter a golden age. In 1859, drilling for oil began and kerosene (a petroleum derivative) soon became widely available for artificial lighting (lamps). But in 1879, Thomas Edison invented the electric light—an incandescent bulb with a carbon filament—which burned one hundred times brighter than kerosene.* Inside homes and shops, the distinction between day and night was overcome. By 1912, 16 percent of American houses had electricity, but by 1927 the proportion had risen to 63 percent. With electricity coursing through their walls, the middle classes began to acquire toasters, washers, refrigerators, and, eventually, televisions and computers.

Such inventions, regardless of where they originated, spread throughout the world. "As in material, so also in intellectual production," Marx wrote. "The intellectual creations of individual nations become common property" (page 68). That circumstance will be more and more true for growing middle classes in places like China and India, especially if the second great globalization that began after the Second World War endures.

—Stephen Kotkin

---

*A. Roger Ekirch, *At Day's Close: Night in Times Past* (New York: Norton, 2005).

SIGNET CLASSICS

Writings from the American Body Politic

The Federalist Papers
Alexander Hamilton, James Madison & John Jay

Edited by Clinton Rossiter, with an Introduction and notes
by Charles R. Kesler

These are some of the most fundamental writings of the American political landscape. Here are the thoughts of the architects of the strong, united government that we have today. This collection contains all eighty-five papers from the edition first published in 1788. It also includes the complete *Constitution*, with marginal notes for relevant passages of the text.

The Anti-Federalist Papers
& the Constitutional Convention Debates

Edited by Ralph Ketcham

While the Federalists supported a strong central government, the Anti-Federalists saw this as a threat to personal freedom and the liberties so hard-won from England. This split, between the desire for local control and the idea of a centralized power, is one of the major causes of the Civil War.

The Declaration of Independence and
The Constitution of the United States

Introduction and Notes by Floyd G. Cullop

The ideal introduction for students, aspiring citizens, and general readers to documents as relevant today as they were when first drafted more than 200 years ago.

Available wherever books are sold or at
signetclassics.com